Personal Development Mastery
2 Books in 1

The Keys to being Brilliantly Confident and More Assertive

+

How to be Charismatic, Develop Confidence, and Exude Leadership

Richard Banks

Personal Development Mastery

Personal Development Mastery

© COPYRIGHT 2020 - ALL RIGHTS RESERVED.

The content contained within this book may not be reproduced, duplicated or transmitted without direct written permission from the author or the publisher.

Under no circumstances will any blame or legal responsibility be held against the publisher, or author, for any damages, reparation, or monetary loss due to the information contained within this book. Either directly or indirectly.

Legal Notice:

This book is copyright protected. This book is only for personal use. You cannot amend, distribute, sell, use, quote or paraphrase any part, or the content within this book, without the consent of the author or publisher.

Disclaimer Notice:

Please note the information contained within this document is for educational and entertainment purposes only. All effort has been executed to present accurate, up to date, and reliable, complete information. No warranties of any kind are declared or implied. Readers acknowledge that the author is not engaging in the rendering of legal, financial, medical or professional advice. The content within this book has been derived from various sources. Please consult a licensed professional before attempting any techniques outlined in this book.

By reading this document, the reader agrees that under no circumstances is the author responsible for any losses, direct or indirect, which are incurred as a result of the use of the information contained within this document, including, but not limited to, — errors, omissions, or inaccuracies.

Personal Development Mastery

The Keys to Being Brilliantly Confident and More Assertive 13

Introduction 15

Chapter 1: What Does It Mean to Be Assertive? 21

What Is Assertiveness? 21

Assertiveness Is a Skill, Not a Personality Trait 22

The Benefits of Assertiveness 27

Why Many People Struggle with Assertiveness 29

How Assertiveness Is Linked to Self-Esteem 32

Chapter 1 Summary 36

Chapter 2: Communication Styles 37

What Is Communication? 38

Verbal Communication 40

Nonverbal Communication 42

Body Language 47

The 4 Communication Styles 54

Outcomes of the 4 Communication Styles 59

How To Use Different Communication Styles In Different Situations 63

How to Be Aware of Your Own Communication Style 64

Chapter 2 Summary 65

Chapter 3: Self-Evaluation 67

Core Values - What Are They? 69

How to Get In Touch With Your Core Values 70

The Benefits of Getting in Touch with Your Core Values 74

Your Vision for Yourself 75

How to Get in Touch with Your Vision for Yourself 77

How Assertive Are You? 79

How You Are Viewed By Others 82

How You Are Viewed By Yourself 88

How Understanding This Can Benefit You 101

Chapter 3 Summary 103

Chapter 4: Obstacles to Assertiveness 105

Common Obstacles People Face When trying to Communicate Assertively 106

Chapter 4 Summary 121

Chapter 5: The Benefits of Assertiveness 123

Top 10 Benefits of Being Assertive 123

The Benefits to an Assertive Communication Style 124

Drawbacks of the Three Other Communication Styles 127

Chapter 5 Summary 130

Chapter 6: Reprogram Your Mind for Success 133

How to Be Clear About Your Intentions and Your Vision 133

Setting Goals to Build Assertiveness 135

How to Set Goals to Build Assertiveness Using SMART Goal Setting 136

What Is SMART Goal Setting? 137

The Benefits of Positive Thinking and Positive Self-Talk 142

How to Put This into Practice 146

A Note on Using Visualization 157

How to Reprogram Your Mind to Be More Assertive 164

What Is Self-Confidence? 164

The Value of Stepping Out of Your Comfort Zone 167

How Stepping Out of Your Comfort Zone Relates to Self-Confidence 169

Tips to Build Self-Confidence 173

How to Reprogram Your Mind to Be More Confident 174

Chapter 6 Summary 183

Chapter 7: How to Be More Assertive 185

Tips to Be More Assertive 185

Strategies for Being More Assertive 190

What Does Effective Communication Look Like? 218

Tips to Be a More Effective Communicator 220

Exercises to Practice Assertiveness 225

Chapter 7 Summary 226

Chapter 8: Being Assertive at Work 227

The Benefits of Assertiveness at Work 227

The Relationship Between Workplace Stress and Assertiveness 230

The Art of Being Assertive in the Workplace 231

How to Deal with Difficult or Narcissistic Bosses or Co-Workers 232

How to Manage Staff Assertively 235

Managing Customer Relationships Assertively 237

How to Ask for a Pay Raise 238

Chapter 8 Summary 241

Chapter 9: Assertiveness in Relationships 243

Different Kinds of Relationships 244

The Importance of Being Assertive in Relationships 248

How to Be Assertive Without Being Aggressive 249

Benefits of Being Assertive in a Relationship 250

Tips for Being Assertive in a Relationship 253

Chapter 9 Summary 256

Chapter 10: Assertiveness for Women Error! Bookmark not defined.

The Importance of Assertiveness for Women 257

Challenges Women Face When Being Assertive 259

Strategies for Women 261

Chapter 10 Summary 264

Conclusion Error! Bookmark not defined.

How to be Charismatic, Develop Confidence, and Exude Leadership 269

Introduction 271

Chapter 1: Making First Impressions 277

Why Are First Impressions Important? 277

How to Radiate Authentic Positivity for a Great First Impression 279

Master the Art of Asking and Answering Questions 286

Summary 288

Chapter 2: Confidence and Mindset 291

How to Build Rock-Solid Confidence 291

How to Boost Confidence 293

Exercises That Help You Eliminate Self-Doubt 295

How to Go from Nervous to Confident in Less Than Two Minutes 297

How to Solidify Confidence and Don't Clam Up in Social Gatherings 299

Positive Thinking and Positive Self-Talk 300

How to Improve Your Self-Image 302

Believe in Your Worth 304

Summary 306

Chapter 3: The Power of Listening and Remembering names For Magnetic Charisma 309

Why You Need Interpersonal Skills to Become Charismatic 310

Learn How to Remember People's Names 313

How to Be a Good Listener 316

Summary 318

Chapter 4: How to Small Talk 321

How to Improve Your Small-Talk Skills 322

How to Lead Conversations to Connect and Spread Your Influence 324

How to Keep Conversations Going to Avoid Awkward Pauses 326

How to Improve Conversation Skills for Memorable Conversations 327

Summary 329

Chapter 5: Storytelling 333

Why You Need to Be a Good Storyteller 333

How to Tell a Convincing Story 335

How to Make Your Story Memorable 338

How to Tell Personal Stories 341

Summary 342

Chapter 6: Presence and Magnetism 345

Strategies for Growing Magnetic Charisma 346

How to Influence People with Your Magnetic Presence 349

How to Speak so That You Command Attention 352

Summary 356

Chapter 7: Being Assertive 357

Develop Social Assertiveness and Get What You Need and Want Out of Interactions 357

Assertiveness Isn't a Personality—It's a Skill 358

How to Start Training to Be Assertive 360

Techniques and Exercises for Assertiveness 366

Summary 370

Chapter 8: Being a Charismatic Leader 373

How to Motivate Others to Be Excited About Doing What You Persuade Them to Do 373

How to Quickly Read Anyone and Know What Triggers Will Influence Them 381

How to Become Influential 382

Summary 385

Chapter 9: Group Interactions 387

Group Interaction Skills for Charismatic Leaders 388

Summary 393

Chapter 10: Handling Conflicts Error! Bookmark not defined.

Types of Conflict and the Best Ways to Find a Solution 397

Why Conflict Occurs? 398

Best Ways to Manage a Conflict 400

Conflict-Solving in Leadership 401

How to Resolve Personal Conflicts to Sway People on Your Side 404

Summary 408

Conclusion Error! Bookmark not defined.

References 417

Personal Development Mastery

The Keys to Being Brilliantly Confident and More Assertive

A Vital Guide to Enhancing Your Communication Skills, Getting Rid of Anxiety, and Building Assertiveness

Richard Banks

Personal Development Mastery

Introduction

All of us can think of times when we know we should speak up, but we don't. When we feel like we're being taken advantage of, but we just accept it. Later, we kick ourselves, thinking: "If only I would have *said something!*"

This book will help you if you are a person who feels like you need to increase your assertiveness, to improve your communication skills, to better deal with conflict, to improve your level of confidence and to be a better leader. In this book, you will learn how to improve all of these skills and more!

The purpose of this book is to serve as a complete guide to help you understand what assertiveness is and how you can become more assertive in your own life. Using practical exercises and techniques will teach you how to stand up for what you believe, ask for what you want and need, and say no to what you don't want in a way that's confident, calm, and respectful. This book will also be your guide for increasing self-confidence and self-worth. By reading this book, you will improve your life, gain more control over your life, improve your communication skills and your interpersonal skills and be more successful in both your personal life and your work life.

Before we begin delving into how you can start to take action, we are going to look at an important theory related to changing oneself. This theory comes down to your mindset. The type of mindset that you employ has a massive impact on your life and your growth as a person. There is something called a Growth Mindset, which is an essential piece of this book and your goals of changing yourself. The **'growth mindset'** is a term that was coined by Carol Dweck, who is a renowned professor at multiple universities, including Columbia University, Harvard University, and the University of Illinois. Her research with Angela Lee Duckworth stated that intelligence is not a key indicator of success. They believed that success depends on whether or not a person has a *growth mindset*. A **'fixed mindset'** is the opposite of a growth mindset. A fixed mindset is a term for when a person believes that their intelligence and skills are fixed traits and that they are not able to be changed. People of this mindset believe that they have what they have, and that's it.

Knowing this fact and the proof it provides can help you to feel empowered and hopeful. If you struggle with your confidence and your level of assertiveness, understanding that it is a skill that can be learned and honed over time means that this will not remain something that you struggle with anymore. By picking up this book, you are already taking the first steps involved in changing your life by becoming a more confident and more assertive person. If this were an innate characteristic, this would mean that it would be difficult for you to change. Take comfort in this fact and continue reading this book as we will discuss exactly how you can make these changes in your life.

By the end of this book, you will be well on your way to changing your life for the better in numerous ways, and you will be wondering how you ever lived without this information. There is no better time than now to change the parts of yourself that you wish were different, so don't wait, read on to chapter one now!

Personal Development Mastery

Chapter 1: What Does It Mean to Be Assertive?

To begin, we are going to look at what assertiveness is, as well as some points related to assertiveness so that you can get a better idea of what exactly this word means. By first making sure that you understand assertiveness, this will help you to understand what benefits can come of assertiveness and how it will benefit you.

What Is Assertiveness?

Assertiveness is being able to use effective communication as well as negotiation, in order to remain true to your personal needs and boundaries when interacting with other people. Being assertive isn't about aggressively putting up walls and shutting people out, contrary to popular belief. There is no shame in being assertive; it is quite a valued skill both in a person's personal life and in their work or professional life.

Assertiveness Is a Skill, Not a Personality Trait

Assertiveness, communication, conflict resolution, confidence, and leadership. What do all of these have in common? All of these are skills and not innate characteristics. What does this mean? I will start by defining these two terms for you. A learned skill, as I am sure you can imagine, is something that you can learn and develop in order to possess. This is the opposite of an innate characteristic, which is something that you are born with. For instance, the color of your eyes or certain aspects of your personality, such as being stubborn.

Skills are things that you can study, practice, and improve upon. Skills are things like communication or cooking. On the other hand, a characteristic is something that you possess that you do not have much control over. You can work on things like becoming less stubborn, but for the most part, you are born a stubborn person, or you are not.

Remember, in the introduction to this book when we discussed the differences between a *fixed mindset* and a *growth mindset*? This comes into play here once again, as you must check your mindset before setting out to make changes. Having a fixed mindset makes a person highly concerned with what skills and intelligence they currently have, and those that they were born with, and it does not allow them any room to focus on what they can develop or improve upon. Therefore, their activities are limited to the capacity that they think they have.

However, those with growth mindsets understand that skills and intelligence are something that can be developed and learned throughout the course of their life. This can be done through reading, education, training, mentorships, or simply just passion. They understand that their brain is a muscle that can be 'worked out' to grow stronger. Knowing this, you must employ a growth mindset. Every single skill you have, as well as your intelligence and confidence, can be improved or changed by putting in the effort to do so. Famous public figures of success like Oprah Winfrey, Steve Jobs, and Bill Gates all employed a growth mindset, which allowed them to overcome every obstacle that got in their way. Rather than succumbing to defeat, they worked and discovered innovative ways to overcome previous failures and found success at the end.

Think about what mindset you have right now. If you already have a growth mindset, you simply need to continue practicing it while being proactive about dealing with obstacles and overcoming failures. If you think you are someone with a fixed mindset, you must change it right now. Believe me when I tell you that confidence and skills such as assertiveness can be improved upon with time and hard work, and this book will show you how. If you don't believe me, just try it. Pick a random skill; this could be knitting, computer programming, jogging, or anything that can be learned. Set goals for yourself and begin learning something new. If you can take something that you have zero skill in and become proficient in it, you have just proved to yourself that growth mindsets are real and fixed mindsets only hold you back from success. This is proof that the only thing holding you back from becoming a more assertive and confident you, is your mindset.

Take some time to consider this and evaluate yourself and your mindset before moving on, as it will play a vital part in your success throughout this book and life.

The Benefits of Assertiveness

There are numerous benefits to assertiveness, many of which you are likely aware of, or you would not have opened this book in the first place. In this section, we will look at some of the most valuable benefits of being an assertive person.

- Being assertive allows you to communicate in a confident and clear way
- Being assertive allows you to practice self-care by setting boundaries and sticking to them
- Being assertive allows you to deal with conflict in your personal and professional lives most effectively and maturely possible

- Being assertive allows you to share your ideas and thoughts persuasively and calmly, which will command attention and respect
- Being assertive allows you to ensure your needs are being met
- Being assertive allows you to feel comfortable and confident, saying "no."
- Being assertive helps you to provide feedback to others in a constructive and effective way
- Being assertive improves your interpersonal skills
- Being assertive helps you to be more confident in yourself and your decisions and ideas
- Being assertive helps you to reduce your stress levels by helping you to

confidently prioritize your time and energy
- Being assertive increases your self-respect, self-confidence, and self-worth
- Being assertive helps you to be a better negotiator
- Being assertive helps you to remain calm under pressure

Why Many People Struggle with Assertiveness

One of the main reasons that people struggle with being assertive is because it is a means to protect oneself. A person may not even realize that they are doing this to protect themselves, and they may genuinely want to be more assertive. Still, many people have trouble with this because the avoidance of being assertive helps a person feel as though they are in control of their life by avoiding the possibility of negative emotions. This is what is called a defensive measure. Defensive measures are actions that a person takes to avoid getting hurt or to minimize the risk of getting hurt. External defensive behaviors are a type of defensive measure that is used to help a person prevent harm or conflict with other people. This includes being non-assertive, being submissive, silencing yourself, blaming yourself, and keeping distance between yourself and others. This is a common reason that people have a lack of assertiveness, and it is something that we will address heavily in this book.

Behind this effort to avoid getting hurt, there could be many reasons. The most common reasons begin in childhood, believe it or not. Our upbringing and childhood experiences typically play a massive role in your level of self-esteem in your adult life. Did you grow up in a strict family who barely ever gave you praise? Did a more successful sibling always overshadow you? Did you grow up in a family where nobody was ever around, and you were left to fend for yourself? These are all examples and reasons why people may have lower self-esteem compared to others. Studies show that children who were raised in families or households where love was not often shown or expressed, typically had lower levels of self-esteem later in life when compared to children that were shown love or who grew up in families where love was expressed.

Further, in an incredibly fast-paced society with the obsessive usage of social media, it is so difficult not to compare ourselves to others.

Have you ever found yourself obsessively stalking or following a celebrity's Instagram page? Are you continually following people who became millionaires at the ripe age of 22? Or are you following gorgeous models who have the world's population fiending for them? In this day and age, our exposure to hotter, wealthier, and more successful people are continuously growing. Seeing incredible success like this every day really makes it hard for you to recognize your self-worth and, in turn, lowers your self-esteem.

How Assertiveness Is Linked to Self-Esteem

When people have a healthy level of self-esteem, they typically have a positive outlook on themselves. They believe in their capabilities to achieve goals and do not spend a lot of time dwelling on failure. They are not afraid to ask for help from others to help them reach their goals. They are also able to be assertive and be able to say "no" to situations or requests that they do not want to do.

Having a healthy level of self-esteem helps increase assertiveness because you believe in what you are saying and doing. If you believe that you need or want something, you won't spend time dwelling on whether you think other people think it is true, you will just ask for it. Those who have low self-esteem typically suffer from not being able to ask for what they need or want because they are afraid of being judged or rejected. In their minds, asking for something for 'need' is a sign of weakness, and therefore, people will judge them for asking for it.

On the flip side, somebody with a healthy level of self-esteem typically isn't afraid of that because that hasn't even crossed their mind. Since having healthy self-esteem comes from loving yourself and respecting yourself, it feels perfectly reasonable to ask for what they feel like they need and want.

For this reason, self-esteem and assertiveness are inextricably linked, and to work on one, we must work on the other. Throughout this book, you will see how self-esteem and assertiveness play into one another and how they come together in many different situations.

To help you understand further what being assertive means, I will provide you with an example. Imagine if your mother wanted you to come over to her house as soon as possible so you can help her pack up her things to prepare for a move. However, you had planned to spend your evening relaxing, watching a movie, and taking a hot bubble bath because you have had a busy week at work. Assertiveness, in this case, would be valuing your own needs just as much as you value your mother's needs. A person with a healthy amount of self-esteem will be able to demonstrate assertiveness by saying, "I am worthy of this. I deserve my break when I need it." Somebody with low self-esteem will typically think, "It will be selfish of me to take a break when somebody needs my help." A part of having self-esteem is being able to understand that you can't pour from an empty glass. In the example above, those with low self-esteem will go and help their mother move anyway despite being exhausted and end up feeling like other people do not respect their time and feelings. In reality, people do not know what you need if you are unable to communicate it. In the next chapter, we are going to look at communication styles and the most effective styles for being assertive and expressing yourself clearly.

Chapter 1 Summary

In this chapter, we discussed assertiveness and the importance of viewing it as a skill rather than a personality trait. We also discussed the importance of the growth mindset and how it will help you in your life.

Chapter 2: Communication Styles

When it comes to being more assertive, understanding communication is essential. In this chapter, we are going to look at communication and how to be an effective communicator. Once you learn this, it will be much easier to work on improving your assertiveness, which is why we are addressing communication so early on in this book. We will begin by looking at what communication is, in its most basic form, and then we will look at different communication styles and when they are most useful.

What Is Communication?

Communication, in its most basic form, is a way of exchanging information with others. There are many ways that we can communicate with others, including verbal and nonverbal methods. In addition, with the advent of technology, a plethora of additional means of communication have been created.

Communication is not only an essential part of our relationships but also our day to day life in general. You will often communicate with people in some way without even having a relationship with them. For example, when you go to the store, you will communicate with the cashier. You may also give a nod or a look to someone else in their car as a form of communication. Communication is essential when living in a society of humans and is even present among other species. Communication has been key to interpersonal connections long before the modern languages we know and use now came about. Being able to communicate effectively is useful for interactions in your workplace, in your home and family life, in your leisure activities, and in your everyday interactions as you move through the world alongside other people.

Everybody has the ability to use basic communication- this propensity for verbal communication is something that humans are born with, which is why we are able to learn languages with such ease as babies. This does not mean, however, that everybody can communicate effectively or with skill. The most basic level of communication involves things like being able to speak simple words and phrases and being able to recognize and tell someone what your basic needs are (such as being hungry or having to go to the bathroom). Basic communication also includes being able to hear what another person is saying to you and understanding what it means at a surface level.

Verbal Communication

Verbal or oral communication uses spoken words to communicate a message. Within verbal communication, there are different types. We are going to look at these types in more detail.

Intrapersonal communication is a type of communication that only involves oneself. This can also be referred to as "silent conversations with ourselves." It comes in the form of thoughts and ideas and goes on within your mind consciously or subconsciously. We use this type of communication, while making decisions about our actions or thinking about concepts. We will often switch back and forth between the listener and the speaker during this type of communication as we are, in a way, bouncing ideas off of ourselves. This type of communication can remain intrapersonal if not shared with others, or it can become the next type of communication that we will look at if we then decide to verbalize it with others.

This next form of verbal communication is called Interpersonal communication. While the words intrapersonal and interpersonal seem similar at first glance, their meaning is different. Interpersonal communication means communication between two people. This typically occurs with two individuals having a one-on-one interaction. In this type of communication both persons are the listener and the speaker, and they will switch back and forth between roles depending on who is speaking.

Nonverbal Communication

Communication can be taken much further than the basics, as there are many small and subtle ways that people communicate their thoughts and feelings without saying a word. Being able to pick up on these types of communications while interacting with someone is what sets basic communication apart from effective and intelligent communication.

This type of communication is called nonverbal communication.

Nonverbal communication influences a large percentage of what humans base their first impressions of others on. Because of this, it is essential to understand what the things we see are telling us about another person, and what we may be telling others through our own body language.

First, though, what exactly do we mean when we say nonverbal communication? This term includes a wide variety of ways that people communicate without using words. This involves things that people do (or do not do) that send messages about what they think and feel. Humans are quite selective about what they choose to share with others. They choose when and whom to share information with, but their bodies sometimes tell a different story. This type of physical, bodily communication can be either a conscious or unconscious action, meaning that we may not even be aware that we are sharing our thoughts, feelings, or opinions in ways other than through our words. It is essential to understand this concept because of what messages you may be sending and also what others may be saying without being aware of it.

One example of nonverbal communication is the use of vocal dynamics. Vocal communication may seem similar to verbal communication; however, there is a lot more to a sentence than the words it contains. The way that someone delivers a sentence is much more telling than the words it contains. For example, the inclusion of a pause or a drawn-out word and even complete silence can tell you about a person's internal state. If a person becomes suddenly silent, they may be offended by the topic of conversation or by something that was said. If the person avoids silence at all costs, they are likely a nervous or anxious person who is uncomfortable with a silent moment or two. The tone of voice and volume play a critical part in this as well. If you didn't understand a word that someone was saying but could read their nonverbal communication cues, you would be able to tell a lot about what they were trying to convey. Like facial expressions, this is another type of nonverbal communication that we learn when we are very young. We can tell the difference between a happy and an angry sentence even before we have a full vocabulary to use and understand the meaning of the sentence. The volume of a person's voice can also indicate traits of their personality or their current state. If they are speaking very quietly, they are probably shy or nervous, while a loud volume can mean that they are angry or excited. A great example of the tone of a person's voice demonstrating more than what their words are saying is sarcasm. When we are using sarcasm, the tone of our voice is precisely the opposite of what we are saying. The message we are trying to convey is not evident in the words we are saying, but rather the tone in which we are saying them. If someone were to misunderstand our tone, they could become perplexed as to what we meant. If we say, "I loved waiting in line for four hours," the tone we say it with indicates that we actually mean exactly the opposite. By choosing the appropriate vocal dynamics, you can convey assertiveness.

Body Language

Body language is a fairly broad term and can include a variety of different forms of nonverbal communication, such as hand gestures and facial expressions, but also includes things like touch and head movements.

Body language can be conscious or unconscious. Most of us are very familiar with conscious body language as we more than likely use this as a form of communication on a regular basis.

An example of a deliberate display of body language would be the use of hand signals. These vary between cultures and regions of the world, but every culture has some. They may change with changes in pop culture, or they may be long-standing such as the thumbs up in

North America. These hand signals are a form of body language that we use to convey specific messages to others.

Another example is a handshake. A handshake is a nonverbal way of saying that you are welcoming someone to make contact with you and is a friendly greeting upon meeting someone new.

Another example of conscious body language is facial expressions. There are many facial expressions that we consciously make to convey messages to people. Facial expressions can express anger, sadness, or happiness. Humans often make these facial expressions to tell others how they feel without speaking. Have you ever been with your partner in a situation where they said something that frustrated you, and you gave them a specific look to let them know that they have upset you? With this one simple facial expression, they know what you are thinking and feeling.

We will now look at unconscious body language in terms of different areas of the body. We will examine all of these different areas and what they may be telling us by their actions. The face is where we will begin. The face is very involved when it comes to deciphering nonverbal communication because it has so much to tell us. There are many different places to look for clues on the face.

The Eyes

Firstly, the eyes. Our eyes operate significantly on their own accord- blinking when they need to and gazing where there is movement. While we can most often control where they look, they will sometimes operate on their own in interactions with others. The eyes will often be the first place to show how the person is feeling. Our brain and our spinal cord make up the pairing that is known as the central nervous system. This pathway of neurons operates fully automatically- that is to say, with no help from our conscious mind. The eyes are connected to this nervous system and are the only part of the system that faces the outside of the body. Because of this, the eyes are intertwined with what we are thinking and feeling, even more than we notice. The brain and the spinal cord give us life- they are responsible for initiating our movements, our thoughts, and our feelings. "The eyes are the window to the soul" got its origins in this fact of anatomy. It is very difficult to control the emotions and sentiments that people can see in our eyes as they come directly from the places within us over which we have no control. The eyes, therefore, are the first place to look when it comes to seeing someone's truth.

Eye contact is a significant indicator of the intentions of a person. As previously discussed, the amount of eye contact someone is making is an indicator of their level of comfort. If someone is making and holding eye contact for an extended period of time without looking away, they appear to be very comfortable to the point of seeming like they may have predetermined intentions. If someone is avoiding eye contact altogether, they tend to seem very untrustworthy, almost as if they are trying very hard to hide something from you. We have all encountered an uncomfortable amount of eye contact, whether too much or too little, where it made us feel like something was not right. You may have been feeling unease but were unaware as to why. Feeling someone's eyes staring directly into yours with no end in sight makes for a lot of discomfort, while trying to catch someone's eye who is clearly making an effort to avoid yours makes for a very awkward conversation. If someone is making steady eye contact, looking away now and then, and then coming back to meet your eyes once again, they are probably feeling comfortable in the situation or conversation and are quite secure with themselves and their position. This amount of eye contact makes us feel comfortable in the other person's presence and think that their intentions are pure.

The Arms

The arms themselves can close us off or open us up to the world. The positioning of the arms in relation to the body can be something that happens automatically. Someone may be extremely comfortable with the situation they are in if they have their arms at their sides, or resting on the armrests of the chair in which they are seated. This may happen automatically as a result of feeling unthreatened and safe in their surroundings.

Arms behind the back indicate that the person is feeling secure and welcoming a challenge. We know this because they have their protecting elements (their arms) behind them and their chest out and exposed, meaning that they will not be able to quickly protect themselves if need be. This is an indication of feeling secure and comfortable or feeling like they are stronger than those around them.

There are even more places to look for body language cues, some of which we will examine in more detail later on in this book when we look at how to read a person and how you can exhibit assertive body language.

The 4 Communication Styles

As you now know, communication comes in many different forms, but in this case, we are going to look at different styles of verbal communication. There are four styles of verbal communication that we will examine. They are as follows.

Aggressive Communication Style

The first communication style we will explore is

the Aggressive Communication Style. This communication style is borne out of a place of fear. This person fears they will not be heard or understood, and therefore, they enter into interaction or conversation with a loud volume and an attitude of entitlement. They approach the conversation with a wide stance and a confrontational posture. They feel the need to shout over others and force their point of view. This style of communication can often end up having the exact effect the communicator is trying to avoid, which is that people may not end up listening to the content of the sentences because they are distracted by the way that it has been conveyed. When people are faced with an aggressive communication style, they tend to become defensive and closed-off, unwilling to engage much further in the interaction.

Passive Communication Style

The second is the Passive Communication Style. This type of communicator prefers to avoid conflict at all costs. They would rather please people than to make their opinion known. They are easily swayed, and they tend to speak with a very low volume. They attempt to shrink themselves down using their body language with hunched shoulders and crossed arms. They feel as if their opinions are not valid and are apologetic if they think that someone disagrees with them. Other people will approach this type of communicator in an exasperated manner as they feel that they have to walk on eggshells in an effort to preserve the person's feelings.

Passive-Aggressive Communication Style

The next is the Passive-Aggressive

Communication Style. These types of communicators initially show one type of attitude on the outside, that their words do not match. They use passive, self-shrinking body language, therefore, appearing to be submissive and non-confrontational on the outside, while communicating with their words in an aggressive manner. It is the combination of both of the previous two styles of communication. They tend to speak aggressively to indirectly make a point but act out passively in front of the person. Their words are of an aggressive nature, but they deliver them in a passive style. They will use a low volume and a gentle tone while saying something likely to cause confrontation or to make someone angry. People tend to become frustrated when dealing with this type of communicator because there is a lot of close attention that needs to be paid to figure out what exactly they are trying to say. It is often used by people who wish to be of an aggressive style but who are afraid to speak out in such a way.

Assertive Communication Style

The final verbal communication style is the Assertive Communication Style. This style of communication is rooted in confidence and self-assuredness. People who communicate in this way have confident body language and maintain eye contact; they are relaxed but engaged. They are emphatic but maintain a normal volume and tone of voice. They are secure in their stance both literally and figuratively and are unafraid of rejection or a disagreeing party. They communicate their points with a calm but firm demeanor.

This type of communicator is the easiest to communicate with as they are able to remain level-headed in disagreement and are not forceful in any way. They are not trying to enforce an attitude of superiority, nor are they trying to stay hidden. They stand in interaction as they are and are not trying too hard to be anything that they are not. People respect the fact that this communicator is able to speak their truth concisely and directly without being aggressive.

Outcomes of the 4 Communication Styles

Each of these different communication styles will result in a different outcome. It is essential to understand these outcomes so that you can choose your method of communication wisely and so that you can see how some of these communication styles are less desirable. We will begin by looking at the outcomes of each of the four communication styles.

- Aggressive Communication Style: I win you lose
- Passive Communication Style: I lose you win
- Passive Aggressive Communication Style: I lose you lose
- Assertive Communication Style: I win you win

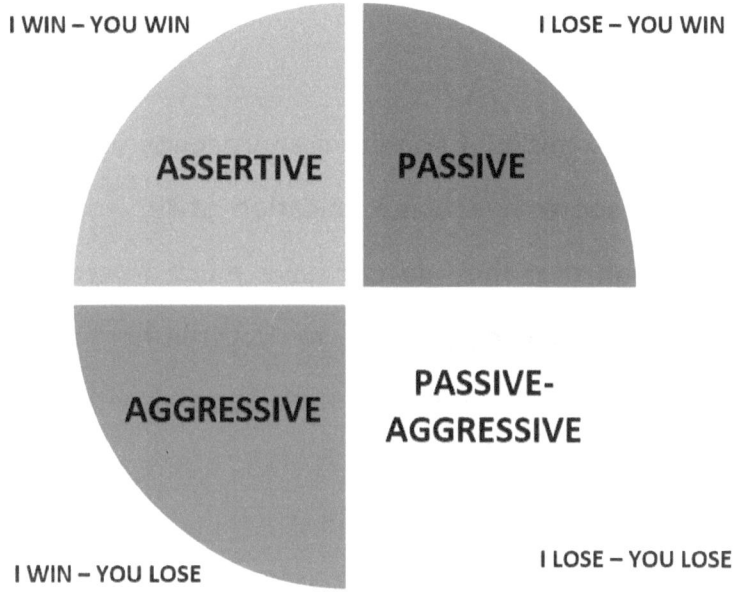

As you can see, each of these styles results in a different outcome, and with each outcome, specific feelings, and takeaways for each person. From this, you can see why the assertive communication style is the best choice and why in this book, we are focused on using this communication style in almost every scenario and encounter that you will find yourself in.

For example, if someone approaches you with an aggressive communication style, you can glean that they do not have much interest in what you may have to contribute to the discussion and maybe quite forceful with their words.

They are interested in "winning" themselves and are intent on having you "lose." Knowing the different styles and how to recognize them can help you to avoid being offended and hurt if someone approaches you in this way and can also help you to determine how to respond appropriately.

How To Use Different Communication Styles In Different Situations

Some of these communication styles may be more effective than others in different situations. There may be some situations where communicating more passively is required, and some situations in which a more balanced, assertive style is the best choice.

Being aware of the different styles and how they sound and look (in terms of body language) can help you to choose which one to use and when depending on the situation and with whom you are interacting. All of these communication styles come with their own characteristic body language, which can help you to identify them. Understanding this can help you to determine which style is being used when communicating with others, as well as which styles others are using to communicate with you.

How to Be Aware of Your Own Communication Style

We may all exhibit a combination of all of these styles but can usually pin ourselves down to one style the majority of the time. Understanding this about ourselves will aid us in communicating our thoughts and ideas more effectively but will also help us in being better able to receive and understand the communication of others' feelings and ideas. Being honest with ourselves and recognizing which style we use the most can help us to analyze our interactions and see why people may react to us in one way or another. Awareness is the key to changing anything, and choosing the most effective communication style will allow you to see other people's true personalities instead of seeing their reaction to your choice of communication style.

To examine your communication style, it is best to examine your body language, your tone of voice, and your choice of words. It is also important to examine how all of these are working together as a whole. By doing this, you will be able to determine your communication style and then decide whether it is effective or if you should work on changing this.

Chapter 2 Summary

The main takeaway from this chapter is the importance of nonverbal communication and how it differs from verbal communication, as well as the four communication styles and the differences between them.

Personal Development Mastery

Chapter 3: Self-Evaluation

In this chapter, we are going to look at several ways that you can self-evaluate. First, though, we are going to look at the importance of self-awareness and why you should spend time on self-awareness in the first place.

To put it simply, self-awareness is being aware of the 'self.' The self is what makes our identity unique. All its unique components include experiences, thoughts, and abilities. Psychologists have concluded that when we focus our attention on our inner selves, we can evaluate and compare our current behavior to the standards and values we hold for ourselves. We become self-conscious and become objective evaluators of our actions as they relate to the core values we hold.

It's essential to recognize that self-awareness is not only about noticing things within ourselves but also how we view our inner world. For example, have you ever judged yourself on the thoughts or experiences you've had? If so, you are not the only person. However, it is time to begin working on a non-judgmental reflection of yourself. If being non-judgmental is a crucial component of self-awareness, how do we begin to work towards that?

As we start to notice what is happening inside of us, we can acknowledge them and accept it as an inevitable part of being human. We should do this rather than giving ourselves a hard time for our mistakes. It is important to remember this as you make your way toward improving yourself and becoming a more assertive individual because making mistakes along the way is inevitable.

Core Values – What Are They?

Our personal beliefs and values profoundly affect our present mindset. If you remember from the first chapter of this book, your mindset plays a significant role in your ability to succeed at making changes to your skills, including the skill of being assertive. Therefore, you must get in touch with your personal beliefs and values, otherwise known as your core values.

Take a look at yourself; what are your current

personal beliefs? Self-awareness is crucial here. You must tap into your self-awareness to be able to identify what your beliefs are. Only when we can identify what our beliefs are, we can change the ones that aren't helping us or shift the ones that we wish to change.

How to Get In Touch With Your Core Values

Getting in touch with your core beliefs will also help you in being more assertive, as you will then be able to speak up about what your core beliefs are and ensure that your needs are being met.

Knowing how to listen to your feelings is vital in being able to begin understanding your own personal core values. For many people, this is a challenge. We live in a culture where concentration, looking inward, and getting in touch with the deeper parts of yourself, is not as valued as multitasking and handling distractions. This is due, in large part, to the media and consumerism, where we are constantly bombarded with information. For this reason, short-focus sessions that allow a person to tune out of life for a moment can prove to be very refreshing. Looking inward and getting in touch with your feelings will take practice and dedication, but once you get used to it, it will become more comfortable for you. Having this connection with yourself will help you to express yourself assertively in your relationships. This cannot happen without an understanding of your feelings, your needs, and your core values.

In addition to practicing listening inward to your

feelings, another way to get in touch with your core values is to pay attention to the deeper needs that your feelings may be alerting you to.

For example, if you feel an emotion and you look inward, say you come to the conclusion that you are feeling betrayed. Betrayal is the feeling or emotion that you are experiencing. You will then need to try to understand what core value or more deep-seated need this feeling is associated with. You will need to spend some time with yourself and try to determine the need that is not being met based on your own personal values.

To do this, look at the situation that you find yourself in for clues. For example, a close friend of yours tells someone some information that you told them in confidence, leaving you feeling betrayed. In response to this feeling, you must then think to yourself, "what personal need is being unmet?" There are different possibilities, and it is up to you as the individual who is feeling betrayed to determine what need or value this is associated with. It could be that you value friendship, and thus you feel betrayed because your friend lied to you. It could also be that you need or value personal security, and that has been jeopardized as a result of this situation.

Each time you recognize that you feel a negative emotion in a given situation, you can look at the situation along with your emotion and determine what personal need or value has been unmet in that scenario. This will help you to take stock of your core values and your beliefs. Over time, you will gain a better understanding of your values, and which of them are the most important to you.

After you determine these, you will be able to express yourself calmly and assertively to ensure that your needs and values are being respected by you and by others in any given situation.

The Benefits of Getting in Touch with Your Core Values

Take a minute to think about some of the things that you value in a relationship. This could be a friendship, a romantic relationship, or a familial relationship. You may appreciate important things like integrity, dependability, loyalty, and honesty. All of these traits require a person to have a strong character. It requires someone who is able to be true and act true to their values and beliefs, even when it would be easier to simply let it go and please other people. This is where assertiveness comes in, as you must be assertive to stand up for these things, which you value to take care of yourself and your needs. By understanding these values, you can then benefit yourself by ensuring that you do not compromise them.

Your Vision for Yourself

In this section, we are going to look at your vision for yourself. We will begin by looking at the difference between a vision and a goal. Many people mistake their goals and their visions for being the same thing. They will set a goal without thinking about what the goal will allow them to do, be, or have, in the long-term.

To maximize your results in this section, and the

results that you see as a result of your goal-setting process, try to imagine the positive changes that achieving your goals would bring to your life. What would reaching your goals mean for you?

For clarity, let's talk a little bit more about the differences between a person's vision and their goal.

A person's vision isn't something that needs to be created from scratch; in fact, it is something that already exists within them. An example of this would be your vision of yourself as an assertive person with high self-esteem who takes care of themselves by remaining true to their values and beliefs. You simply need to get in touch with it, as it already exists within you. A person's vision is the big picture of their desired outcomes and how those would affect their life as a whole. It represents the most important things to that person and is often compelling, inspiring, exciting, and filled with many positive emotions when a person thinks about it.

On the other hand, a goal is entirely different from a vision. A goal is something that is specifically and thoughtfully designed that requires you to complete a set of tasks to reach a specific feat; this endpoint is the goal.

How to Get in Touch with Your Vision for Yourself

It may seem difficult at first for you to get in touch with your vision for yourself, but I assure you that this vision is within you, and all you have to do is uncover it. One great way to get in touch with your vision for yourself is through the use of visualization. This helps by allowing you to see an image of yourself that you are proud of within your mind. People who struggle with low self-esteem often have a negative perception of themselves that is inaccurate, and this can lead them to feel completely out of touch with their vision for themselves. Visualization is a great technique to envision yourself, achieving your goals.

To begin, get into a quiet place without distractions. Take deep breaths and get in touch with your inner self. This may be the most challenging part for you, but with practice, it will become easier and more comfortable. Once you are in this state of mind, begin to think about your ideal self. What does this version of yourself look like? What traits or skills does this version of yourself possess? How does this version of yourself look? Try to think about every aspect of this version of yourself in as much detail as possible. When you do this, you will begin to understand how you envision your ideal self and your perfect future, and this will help you to start setting goals to get you there.

How Assertive Are You?

In this section, you will be able to determine your current level of assertiveness, so you can assess where you are now compared to where you want to be in the future. First, we will talk about the different levels of assertiveness.

Highly Assertive

If you are highly assertive, this means that you can stand up for yourself in almost every situation that you find yourself in, successfully resolving conflicts and having your needs met and your beliefs uncompromised.

Highly Aggressive

If you are highly aggressive, you can get what you want, but you only know how to do it by stepping on the needs and the feelings of the other people you are interacting with.

Passive-Aggressive

If you are passive-aggressive, this means that you tend to repress your frustration or your anger most of the time. Then, when you inevitably reach your breaking point, you explode into anger at whoever is in front of you in that moment.

Assertive

Being assertive is the middle point between

aggressiveness and passiveness, and it is said to be the happy medium. There are four characteristics associated with being an assertive person. They are as follows:

1. Standing up for yourself in a way that does not offend or hurt other people
2. Expressing your desires and needs
3. Approaching situations and interactions in a confident manner
4. Communicating effectively

As I mentioned in the first chapter of this book, some people will be naturally more assertive, but it is a skill that can be developed and achieved, rather than a personality trait that is fixed.

In addition to the descriptions above, you can determine your level of assertiveness by taking the free assertiveness test at: www.howassertiveareyou.com

How You Are Viewed By Others
By Nonverbal Communication Clues

Observation of a person's body language is helpful when it comes to understanding what type of person they are.

When trying to determine how you are viewed by others, examining your body language can be extremely helpful in seeing yourself through the eyes of other people. When you interact with people, you send certain messages through your body language, which then influences how they perceive and see you. Your body language is being analyzed all the time, as people use it to gain clues into how comfortable you may be feeling in their presence, or what you may be thinking. We are going to look at some examples of body language so that you can get an idea of what messages you may be sending to others.

Body Language that involves a person shutting themselves out from other people that they are interacting with is a prime example of closed-off body language. For example, a person may cross their arms when they are feeling threatened or hug their chest to protect themselves from the outside world. When people do this, they are attempting to physically put a barrier between themselves and you, whether they know this to be true or not. Our bodies are designed to protect us from danger automatically. Our emotions and feelings signal to our body that there may be a threat and our body acts accordingly. This happens regardless of whether there is a real physical threat, or simply a topic of conversation that is making us uncomfortable. To our brain, it is all the same.

Open body language is the opposite of the previous example, and we will look at what this may mean. If the person is showing you relaxed body language, like a relaxed sitting posture by leaning backward and slouching or showing feelings of being at ease by having their arms open wide, for example, they are comfortable and secure in the interaction. When someone is feeling comfortable and welcoming, they may open their arms and leave themselves fully open to receiving the world.

More importantly than noticing these static body language cues is to notice when these body language cues change during an interaction. If the topic changes, do they become suddenly closed-off by putting a barrier like a laptop or a drink between you and them, or do they begin shifting around in their seat? This is an indication that the conversation has reached a topic they are no longer comfortable with. Noticing body language and especially its changes are the key to be a great listener and observer of the feelings of others. In many cases, the majority of the things that we can interpret from an interaction come from the nonverbal cues.

One key part of nonverbal communication that is often overlooked are the things that people do not say. This is a rather tricky concept when it comes to nonverbal communication because it seems as though it would be considered a form of verbal communication. Still, since it does not actually involve words and is more of an abstract concept, it is part of the nonverbal communication umbrella.

It is just as important to pay attention to what the other person (or people) say as it is to pay attention to what is avoided or left out. That is to say, read between the lines. If the person only talks about something specific or is avoiding certain topics altogether, this can give you information about them. In some instances, the things people do not say can tell us more about them than what they do say. If we had not been listening very carefully, we might not even notice what they left out, or we may not remember if they did or did not mention certain things. Listening intently allows you to be sure that they avoided certain things, and then you can determine what this could mean about them or their thoughts and feelings.

After reading through the above examples of common body language, you can begin to self-evaluate and examine your body language in different situations. This will tell you a lot about how you are being perceived and viewed by others.

By Your Communication Style

Using the descriptions of the four different communication styles in chapter 2, you can do a self-examination to determine what type of communicator you are most often. We may all exhibit a combination of all of these styles overall, but we can usually pin ourselves down to one style the majority of the time. Using the descriptions, try to determine the type of communicator you are. If you are not proud of the style that you use most often, try to avoid judging yourself, and be honest with yourself. Throughout the rest of this book, you will learn how to use an assertive communication style to become a better communicator.

How You Are Viewed By Yourself

Recognizing your level of self-esteem will help you to understand how you are viewed by yourself. This will help you to better understand whether you are holding yourself back from success, or if you feel that you are undeserving of positive change.

Self-esteem is your overall opinion of yourself. When you have a healthy level of self-esteem, you have good feelings about yourself and feel deserving of other people's respect. When you have low self-esteem, you often place less value on your thoughts and opinions. We will begin to discuss how to recognize what your level of self-esteem is so that you know where to begin your work.

Do you have low self-esteem?

When people have low self-esteem, they tend to put a minimal value on their thoughts and opinions. You focus more heavily on your perceived weaknesses and past mistakes, and you do not give your skills the credit it deserves. You continuously believe that other people are more capable and successful than you. You also have difficulties being able to accept positive feedback. You find yourself constantly fearing failure, which, in turn, holds you back from succeeding.

Personal Development Mastery

Here is a checklist of symptoms of low self-esteem. Check off the ones that you have experienced. If you have checked off at least four boxes, it means that you may be a victim of low self-esteem.

- ❏ You have a fear of being alone.
- ❏ You doubt your ability to reach success.
- ❏ You choose the wrong partners.
- ❏ You criticize other people.
- ❏ You become rigid.
- ❏ You feel ashamed.
- ❏ You feel depressed.
- ❏ You always put the needs of other people before your own.
- ❏ You experience anxiety.

If you find that you express a lot of these symptoms, that is okay! We will look at strategies for improving this later on in this book.

Do you have healthy self-esteem?

When people have a healthy level of self-esteem, they typically have a positive outlook on themselves. They believe in their capabilities to achieve goals and do not spend a lot of time dwelling on failure. They are not afraid to ask for help from others to help them reach their goals. They are also able to be assertive and be able to say "no" to situations or requests that they do not want to do.

People with healthy self-esteem typically live a happier life as they are more focused on what they have achieved, and what they are doing to achieve more, rather than focusing on past mistakes or the fear of failure. Due to having good self-esteem, it leads them to also build a higher sense of self-confidence. Being confident usually allows the person to excel in social situations, work, sports, and other life-related tasks. Those with healthy self-esteem make a commitment to please and take care of themselves first before trying to please the world.

Here is a checklist of a few signs of healthy self-esteem. Check off the ones that apply to you. If you have less than four boxes checked off, it is a sign that you may have low-medium self-esteem if you check off four or more, it is a sign that you have high-medium healthy self-esteem.

- ❏ You live with humility.

- You speak the truth as you see it, without fearing rejection or having malicious intent.
- You can deliver a message to someone while separated from personal feelings.
- You can recognize where negative emotions such as anger, fear, or guilt stem from.
- You don't follow others just because others are.
- You believe in your ability and other people's ability to make decisions.
- You take accountability when you commit to doing something.
- You can differentiate between the past and present.

Do you have high self-esteem?

There is a theory of self-esteem that many

people agree with. This theory asserts that some individuals use high self-esteem as a cover-up for low self-esteem.

The difference between high self-esteem and healthy self-esteem is that a person with high self-esteem typically comes off as cocky or conceded. When people encounter a person like this, it is quite evident to them that a person like this does not have a healthy level of self-esteem. Instead of earning the respect of others, having self-esteem that is too high shows people that you do not respect yourself enough, so you need to over-communicate your strengths and skills to others in hopes that they will show you the respect you desire. This is called overcompensation.

Those with high self-esteem are usually

covering up the fact that they actually have low self-esteem. They showcase symptoms that are different than those with low self-esteem, as they are trying to cover up their low level of self-esteem.

For example, those with low self-esteem often do not believe in their ability to accomplish things and therefore shy away from them. Those with overly high self-esteem ALSO don't believe in their ability to accomplish things, and also shy away from them, but they spend much more time telling others how much they are doing and how skilled they are in an effort to appear confident. Do you see the difference?

People with healthy self-esteem do not spend time telling others how great they are and how much they have accomplished. Instead, they speak with confidence if they are conversing about a topic that they have successes in. People with high self-esteem will continuously bring up areas of their life that they can brag about to others to mask their lack of self-esteem in other areas of their life. For example, someone with healthy self-esteem may say, "After three years of training for the half marathon, and failing twice, I finally completed it yesterday! I am now training for the next six months to compete in the full marathon." The person with healthy self-esteem is expressing the work that they put into being successful at their goal without the fear of expressing failure on the way. Their statement falls in the middle of two extremes - extremely negative and extremely positive.

On the other hand, people with high self-esteem may sound something like this; "I trained for a year for the half marathon, and I think I actually could have done it with half the training. I bet the full marathon is easier than what other people think it is!" The difference in this statement is that this person is not admitting that they encountered failures and obstacles along the way, something that is inevitable, and they are comparing themselves to others. Instead of focusing purely on their own goals, they are focused on what other people's training is like, and how they can do it faster and better.

Here is a list of behaviors that people with too high self-esteem may exhibit. Check off the ones that apply to you.

- ❏ You are not taking on projects or opportunities because they seem too "easy," or you deem them as beneath your abilities.
- ❏ You take on too many projects when you know you lack the skills to complete all of them.
- ❏ You notice the distance between you and some of your friends, and you think it could have something to do with being too arrogant.
- ❏ You notice some people seem put off at work, and you suspect it may be due to you acting overly conceited.

- ❏ You find that you are more concerned with your own skills and performance and are not involved with your partner's at all.

If you have checked off a few of these, that is okay! Likely your high self-esteem is coming from a place of low self-esteem. You will be able to do practices to help improve your self-esteem throughout this book.

Now that you have done a self-evaluation, you can begin to see how you are viewed by yourself and how this may be affecting your life, including your ability to make the changes you desire, and improving your level of assertiveness.

How Understanding This Can Benefit You

Self-awareness goes way beyond just gaining knowledge about ourselves; it is also focused on paying attention to our inner state and our level of wellbeing with an open mind and heart. Your mind is exceptional at storing information and memories, including memories of how we most often react to certain situations. These memories form a blueprint of our emotional life. Such information ends up training our minds to respond the same way every time we encounter similar situations in the future.

Being self-aware allows us to be aware of the conditioning and training that has shaped our minds. Understanding this is the stepping stone that you need in order to free your mind from that training and teach it new ways to react and respond to situations. This is especially beneficial in situations of conflict or times of stress, where you would like to be more assertive but find it difficult to react assertively in the moment. Being self-aware will help you to change this for the better and begin to be more assertive.

Additionally, people who are self-aware act consciously rather than passively, and usually have good mental wellbeing and a positive view of life. A scientific study in 2016 studied the parts of self-awareness and the benefits. They found that mindfulness, insight, and self-reflection are all aspects of self-awareness and lead to benefits like; becoming a more accepting person and less emotional burdens. The research also found that self-awareness is a critical trait for people who want to be successful business leaders, for whom being assertive is essential.

So, why should self-awareness matter to you? According to psychologists, self-awareness is the cornerstone to achieving emotional intelligence. The ability to monitor and control your thoughts and feelings from minute to minute is important when trying to understand yourself more, and working to consciously make changes in the ways that you communicate, the ways that you react, and the ways that you interact with others.

Chapter 3 Summary

In this chapter, we discussed core values, how you can get in touch with them, and what their importance is. We also talked about how to determine your level of assertiveness and how you can determine how you are viewed by other people.

Chapter 4: Obstacles to Assertiveness

In this chapter, we are going to look at some of the most common obstacles that people face when trying to be assertive. If you can recognize these obstacles, you will then be able to understand how to combat them. If you can combat them, you will be able to get much closer to reaching your goal of being a more assertive person.

Common Obstacles People Face When trying to Communicate Assertively

Below you will find the most common obstacles that people face when trying to communicate assertively.

1. They Don't Know What They Want

If you do not understand what it is that you want, it will be difficult for you to effectively and clearly communicate your wants and needs to other people. Assertive communication is about expressing yourself calmly and effectively so that you can ensure that you are making yourself a priority. When you do not know what it is that you want, you will be unable to share this with others in an assertive way, and you will be much likely to communicate passively instead.

2. They Are Out of Touch with Their True Emotions

If a person is out of touch with their true emotions, they will have a hard time communicating effectively and calmly in situations where they would benefit most from being assertive. Many people have trouble getting in touch with their emotions because instead of trying to understand them, they determine any emotion to be called anger.

Anger is an emotion that is said to be a manifestation of many other types of emotions. What this means is that when a person feels anger, they are actually feeling something different, or a combination of other emotions. This school of thought says that anger itself is not a genuine emotion. The reasoning behind this is that anger is a type of fuel that helps a person get things done or take action to remedy a situation. At the same time, sadness or disappointment are emotions that could be debilitating and leave you wanting to do nothing but lie in bed and cry. When you are feeling anger, this would be one of those times to look deeper and deeper to find out what you are really feeling. Below, we will look at the other emotions that could manifest themselves as anger.

Another reason that anger is often a manifestation of other emotions is that people often use it to cover up the vulnerability that comes with other emotions such as sadness or fear. When a person is angry or acting out in anger, they appear strong or intimidating, and the majority of people would choose this over appearing "weak" or vulnerable. Sometimes intense feelings of any emotion will quickly be converted to feelings of anger to hide or disguise the genuine feelings.

This may happen so quickly and automatically that the person does not even recognize it. Communication requires a person to work on themselves in many ways, and this is one of them. It is often not as easy as just glancing inside to see what emotion you are feeling but challenging yourself to look deeper and be vulnerable.

Anger is seen as one of the most primal human emotions, as it dates back to the beginning of humans. Anger is present in our emotional range to protect us from perceived threats. This results from the time that humans were hunters and needed to protect their families and their land in times of war and other tribes.

Anger is strongly related to the fight or flight response. This explains why we feel the need to take immediate action when we feel intense anger. "fight" from the fight or flight response does not need to involve a physical altercation but can involve fighting with words as well. Knowing this can help when trying to manage anger, as you can stop and recognize that you do not need to react.

Anger can be the surface emotion but is not the root of the feeling. By asking yourself, "why did this make me angry?" you may find that you are indeed scared and not angry.

By understanding the true emotions that lie behind your anger, you can begin to understand how to express these emotions and the needs that they are related to, in an assertive manner. This will help you to prioritize yourself and your core beliefs and values.

3. They Think Their Needs Don't Matter

Depending on the type of family you grew up in, you may have been raised to feel like you are not valued and that you don't have a voice. In this type of family dynamic, your opinions and wants were not acknowledged or taken seriously. The parents themselves likely did not have or model good relationship skills such as; conflict resolution, healthy boundaries, cooperation, and assertiveness. They may even be abusive, exhibiting behaviors like being controlling, preoccupied, manipulative, interfering, or inconsistent. This, in turn, leads them to shame their children's feelings and personality traits. As a result, the child will feel emotionally abandoned and concludes that he/she is not good enough to be accepted by their parents and that it is their fault. Children that grow up feeling insecure and anxious feel unsafe being themselves and often end up codependent with low self-esteem and a tendency to hide their feelings. If this sounds like you, this book will be able to help you to break free from this and grow into an assertive individual who recognizes the importance of your own needs, no matter what age you are now.

4. They Want to Be Loved at All Costs

Having a healthy level of self-esteem means that you hold a good amount of love and respect for yourself. This means that you won't seek it out in others in an unhealthy way. When people do not feel loved by themselves, they will tend to seek out this love from other people, no matter what it takes. This often involves putting their needs and wants to the side in order to feel loved or appreciated in return. This is harmful to your self-esteem as it is a way of showing yourself that you are not worthy of having your own needs met. If you can work on your level of self-confidence and self-love, you will naturally feel more safe and secure in your relationships because what you see in yourself, others probably see in you too and you will not feel the need to prove this to them.

5. They're Frazzled or Flustered

Often while communicating, especially in times of conflict, people will become flustered or frazzled. This state of mind will lead them to have trouble communicating effectively, and they are unable to communicate their needs assertively. If they instead come across aggressively, the other person likely shuts down and has no interest in their needs. They will likely begin communicating in a way that involves some or all of the following:

- Demeaning
- Threatening
- Judging
- Coercing
- Blaming
- Accusing
- Ridiculing
- Criticizing
- Demanding
- Labeling

For this reason, they have trouble having their

needs met, and their conversation usually does not result in any sort of positive resolution.

6. They're Insecure in Their Abilities

Everybody has at least a handful of things that they don't like about themselves or makes them feel inadequate. The problem arises when a person lets these insecurities take over, to the point that they are unable to speak up for themselves because they are so insecure that they fear they never know what they are talking about, or that they are unworthy of sharing their own opinion.

7. They Have a Fear of Retaliation

People often lie to themselves because they are not strong enough to admit insecurity and vulnerability. Many people try their very best to avoid confrontations with other people, whether they want to admit this fact or not. It all comes down to simply not being ready to speak up for themselves due to the fear of retaliation or confrontation. If you have trouble communicating assertively, this may be the reason why.

8. They Are Afraid That People Will Think Badly of Them or Judge Them

If a person has a lot of history being judged by others, they may develop a deep-seated fear of being judged forever. For this reason, they may be afraid to speak up about their needs or wants for fear of being judged because of them. Think about your past; does this sound like you? If so, now that you recognize this, you can begin to combat it to practice self-care and speak up for yourself.

9. They Were Continually Criticized in The Past by Those Who Played an Important Role in Their Life.

Everything we see as children, we are observing to learn more about people, the world, and how to interact with it. The impact that parental modeling has on the development and future of their children should not be underestimated. If you have ever wondered why you have feelings of low self-confidence or self-esteem, think back on what was modeled for you as a child. Maybe you were ridiculed or shamed when you spoke up or shared your opinion. Perhaps you also saw your parents doing this to each other in their interactions. As a result, you learned to think that your opinions, ideas, or needs are unimportant because of the ridiculing and criticizing.

However, regardless of what you saw and learned as a child, it is not too late to learn how to become more assertive and understand why you have challenges with this first step. Becoming more assertive has the potential to change your life and your relationships.

10. Fear of Saying the Wrong Thing

Some people are terrified to say the wrong thing when they are with others, even to a point where they change their opinions and beliefs based on who they are interacting with. This demonstrates a lack of self-confidence, as this person will never choose to speak up for themselves or seek to have their needs met for fear of saying "the wrong thing." This fear of saying or doing something that may hurt the other person's feelings or that may spark anger or frustration in another person can often lead a person to become quite concerned with everything that comes out of their mouth. One crucial thing to note here, however, is that there is no such thing as "the wrong thing," only *your truth*, which you have a responsibility to yourself to stand up for.

11. Fear of Hurting or Offending Others

This fear is a continuation of the previous example, where a person has a fear of saying the wrong thing. The reason for this fear is usually the fear of hurting or offending people. For this reason, a person may refrain from genuinely expressing themselves as they do not want to hurt or offend others, so they do not communicate assertively. Still, instead, they choose not to correspond at all unless it is in agreement with the other people they are interacting with.

12. Fear Others Will Discover How Little You Know

This fear is rooted in a lack of self-confidence. As I have mentioned throughout this book, a lack of confidence is a significant contributing factor to having struggles with assertiveness. One of the reasons that people may have trouble communicating assertively is because they have a fear of other people thinking that they are less educated or that they are making things up. If you have a lack of confidence, this is a common fear. To combat this roadblock, we must first address the low level of self-confidence that comes with it.

13. Fear That Somebody Will Challenge You

This is yet another fear that is associated with a

low level of self-confidence. If you are not confident in yourself and your abilities, you will likely have a great fear of being challenged, as you may worry that you will not know how to respond to being challenged. If you can develop your self-confidence and self-esteem, you will feel much more secure speaking up for yourself, even if you are challenged in the process. With more confidence, you will believe in what you are saying and doing. If you believe that you need or want something, you won't spend time dwelling on whether you think other people think it is true or not, you will just ask for it and can be confident in it no matter what other people say.

Chapter 4 Summary

In this chapter, we are going to look at the most common challenges that people face when they are trying to communicate assertively. By understanding these, you will be able to determine which of these challenges pose the biggest problem for you.

Chapter 5: The Benefits of Assertiveness

In this chapter, we are going to look at the benefits that come with using an assertive communication style in your life. After reading this chapter, you can be confident that you understand why being assertive is such an important skill to develop and maintain.

Top 10 Benefits of Being Assertive

1. Increases your level of self-confidence and self-esteem

2. Allows you to understand and recognize your feelings
3. Helps you to communicate effectively during times of conflict or confrontation
4. Earns the respect of your peers
5. A higher level of self-love and self-respect
6. Allows you to have your way while maintaining solidarity with others
7. More confidence in your decision-making abilities
8. Better negotiation skills
9. Helps you to become a better leader
10. Helps you to foster better relationships

The Benefits to an Assertive Communication Style

As you learned earlier in this book, there are a few different styles of communication that a person can choose to use in any given situation. Here, we will look at the benefits of the assertive communication style.

Their body language shows self-confidence

The assertive communication style is rooted in confidence and self-assuredness. People who communicate in this way have confident body language, and this body language shows others that they have a comfortable level of self-esteem. The type of body language that they convey includes maintaining eye contact and showing that they are relaxed but engaged in the conversation. They are emphatic but maintain a normal volume and tone of voice. They are secure in their stance both literally and figuratively and are unafraid of rejection or a disagreeing party. Being unafraid of rejection and disagreement is a trait of people who are able to be assertive in any given situation.

They are able to remain calm and direct

They communicate their points with a calm but firm demeanor, which commands respect and shows that they are confident in what they are saying.

They are easy to communicate with

This type of communicator is the easiest to communicate with, as they are able to remain level-headed in disagreements and are not forceful with their point of view in any way.

They are comfortable in their stance

They are not trying to enforce an attitude of superiority, nor are they trying to remain hidden. They stand in interaction as they are and are not trying too hard to be anything that they are not. People respect the fact that this communicator is able to communicate without any façade.

Drawbacks of the Three Other Communication Styles

In this section, we will look at some of the drawbacks that come along with using the three other communication styles: aggressive, passive, and passive-aggressive, so that you can understand how they may hinder you in your interpersonal interactions.

The Aggressive Communication Style

As you learned earlier in this book, the aggressive communication style comes with an attitude of entitlement, and people who use this communication style often do so with a forceful demeanor that leaves others feeling angry or frustrated as a result. For this reason, people often do not respond well to those who use this communication style. If you are trying to get your point across, using this style of communication is not an effective way to do so, as people approached in this way often stop listening, as they feel attacked. If you hope to find understanding and a good listener, you likely will not find it using this communication style.

The Passive Communication Style

This communication style tries to avoid conflict at all costs. It is difficult for this type of communicator to get their point across or to share their opinion with anyone. By trying to please people no matter what, you will never come to a conclusion that you are happy with unless you and the person you are interacting with share the same opinions.

People faced with this communication style end up feeling like they have to walk on eggshells in an effort to preserve your feelings, which then leads them to feel as though they cannot share their opinions either. This leads to fake conversations where both people are hiding their true feelings and opinions. This communication style is not an effective way to resolve issues or find out what other people genuinely think about anything.

The Passive-Aggressive Communication Style

Remember, this kind of communication style is used when a person shows one type of attitude on the outside, but their words convey the opposite attitude. For example, showing that you are passive and shy while speaking as though you are confident and angry.

This communication style is ineffective because you will only end up confusing people, as they do not know whether you are angry or shy, and they will not know how to respond to you. This can then lead them to initiate a confrontation with you, as they are likely to become frustrated when dealing with this type of communication style. This is because they will need to try to discern your true feelings or intentions so that they can figure out what you really mean, regardless of what you are saying.

Chapter 5 Summary

In this chapter, we looked at the many benefits of assertiveness, which will keep you motivated as you begin to improve your level of assertiveness.

Personal Development Mastery

CHAPTER 6: REPROGRAM YOUR MIND FOR SUCCESS

To improve upon your assertiveness, you need to work on making it a new habit in your life. I understand that this can feel very intimidating at first, especially if you are focusing on the entire goal of becoming more assertive all at once. To avoid this daunting feeling, keep it very simple. We are going to look at how you can do this so that you will have the best chances of success.

How to Be Clear About Your Intentions and Your Vision

In order to continue strengthening your

assertiveness, a person must have a clear vision of what goals they are trying to accomplish. They must also have an understanding of what success means to them. If a person doesn't know where they're planning to go, or what accomplishing their goals even entails, it is easy for them to lose their way or to get sidetracked. This is why setting goals and being clear with oneself about what you wish to accomplish is so important.

For this reason, it is essential to set out a long-term vision of yourself. Then, from there, you can set shorter-term goals that will act as milestones along the way.

The downside here is that a person's goal may not initiate those positive and exciting emotions that elicit feelings of inspiration. Goals are more like stepping stones on a path that will lead you to your ultimate end goal, which will then bring you the lifestyle that is much more related to your vision of your future self.

One of the best tips for goal setting is to begin making this new lifestyle a habit. Making your motivation a daily practice will be the best way to achieve your goals on the way to your vision.

Setting Goals to Build Assertiveness

Goal setting is the first action that a person needs to make to reach their goals. The purpose behind setting a goal is so that a person can define specific milestones to support achieving their desired results. In this chapter, we are going to look at how you can set goals that will help you to reach your desired results in terms of becoming more assertive in your day to day life.

Setting goals carefully with focus, momentum, action, and intention is the first step a person needs to take to move from where they are now to where they want to be in the future. However, they need to know where it is that they want to be—the "where" begins with a person envisioning their ideal future.

How to Set Goals to Build Assertiveness Using SMART Goal Setting

Instilling a new habit can feel very intimidating at first, so it is essential to break your bigger goal into smaller, more doable ones. Instead of trying to accomplish one massive goal all at once or to change all of your habits all at once, focus on doing just one thing consistently. This will help you to show yourself that you are capable of making change and that you are beginning to make strides towards your goals. In this section, we are going to look at how you can do this.

What Is SMART Goal Setting?

The most popular and effective way to build your goals is using the SMART goals format. You may be familiar with this concept and probably a bit tired of it as most schools and workplaces ask you to complete this regularly. Although it may seem tired and old, there is a reason that it is still so widely used today. This type of goal setting is extremely helpful in leading you to properly define your goal. SMART is an acronym that stands for Specific, Measurable, Achievable, Resources/Realistic, and Time.

We will now delve into SMART goal setting and

what it is:

Specific

This will help you to make sure that your goals are specific and concise enough that you know exactly what you are working towards with no confusion or ambiguity.

Measurable

This ensures that you have a way of measuring your goals for you to be aware of exactly when you achieve your goals and how far you are from achieving them.

Achievable

This ensures that you set goals that are achievable for you. This means that you are setting goals that take into account where you are starting from and how far you can get in the amount of time you have set out for yourself.

For instance, if you are hoping to lose weight, it would not be achievable to set a goal such as, "I want to lose 10 pounds in one week." There is no healthy way to do this, so this would not be an achievable goal. Since the recommended healthy maximum amount of weight loss is roughly one pound per week, it would be better to set yourself a goal such as to lose 6 pounds in 6 weeks, or something such as this.

Resources / Realistic

This part of the acronym ensures that you have a way of getting the necessary resources that will be required for you to reach your goals. This could be anything from financial support to any other resources that you would need to help you reach your goals. It is important to take this into account so that you can adjust your goals accordingly or so that you can figure out what you need to reach those goals. The second half to this letter in the acronym is that the goals are realistic. This is similar to the "Achievable" step we learned above, but in this case, you must give yourself a reality check to ensure that your goal could actually be achieved and that you will not leave yourself disappointed by setting yourself up for failure.

Time

The final letter in the acronym represents having a timeline in which you want your goals to be met. This will give you the much-needed sense of urgency that will help you to continue making progress toward your goals day in and day out, without feeling as though you have all the time in the world, which could lead you to avoid making progress toward your goals. On the other hand, you do not want to set your goals on a timeline that is too short, as this could lead them to become unrealistic or unachievable if there is too little time for you to take the necessary steps to reach your goals.

Using this acronym to set your goals will help you to ensure that you are setting goals that you can achieve, and that will set you on the path to success by helping you build momentum as you achieve short-term goals on the way to achieving your long-term goals.

For example, make sure the goals that you are setting have a clear and concise purpose. For example, don't use goals like "I want to be rich by the next five years." This goal is too broad for it to have a strong meaning. Instead, you should make a goal that is quantifiable like "I am planning on saving $20,000 by the end of this year". Then, when you have a measurable goal, you can make a plan that makes sense for yourself. In this example, a person can plan to save $2,000 each month for the rest of this year to hit their goal of saving $20,000 by the end of it. They can break down these goals even further and figure out where in their budget they can save money or how they can make more money to accomplish that goal.

The Benefits of Positive Thinking and Positive Self-Talk

When a person is experiencing negative emotions like anxiety, fear, worry, or stress, it is a form of negative visualization. It is an unconscious type of visualization where a person is not aware that they are negatively imagining, but it is still a type of visualization, nonetheless. Every time a person stresses or worries about something, they often suffer from having anxiety or fear about what they think the future holds, they are actually in a moment of negative visualization.

Also, in that moment, the person is rewiring their brain in limiting ways. The same method used for a person's mind to be reprogrammed to foster positive habits; it is also able to be reprogrammed negatively. When a person indulges in the negative worries that they're feeling in the moment, they are building on the existing neural pathways within their brain. Due to this, every time a person envisions something negative, it makes it easier for them to have the same future worries.

A person's negative visualizations can make them feel uneasy or anxious at that moment. A person's subconscious can't tell the difference between a visualization and what the person is actually experiencing. Due to this, the person's brain views those events as if it is happening in real life, which causes the neural networks to be formed in their brain, which creates new beliefs, habits of behaviors and perspectives. In plain English, the person is effectively building new patterns by rewiring their brain to support all the things that they have negatively envisioned. When a person does that, it means they are developing a behavior or skill that is unhelpful. The more often that person thinks about this pattern, the easier it is for their mind to keep replaying that pattern repeatedly until the action of worrying becomes a habit that is triggered when a person faces any level of uncertainty.

In addition to this, when a person worries about certain things, those specific things have a higher chance of manifesting in their daily life. This can lead to feelings of dread, and it can keep people stuck and afraid of being assertive. For this reason, positive thinking and positive self-talk are critical and crucial to your success.

If a person believes that they have a limited amount of willpower, they probably will not be able to surpass those limits. However, if a person does not place a limit on themselves, they are less likely to use up their willpower stockpile before meeting their goals. A person's internal perception about their willpower and self-control plays a massive role in determining how much willpower they have. If a person can remove these obstacles by believing that they have a large stockpile of willpower, and believing in themselves, then they are less likely to drain out there will power compared to someone who believes that they don't have much of it.

How to Put This into Practice

There are a variety of ways that you can begin to put positive self-talk and positive thinking into practice. In this section, we will look at these ways and how you can start to use them to achieve your goals.

Changing Your Perception of Willpower

Try to change your perception of how you see your willpower. Rather than thinking of it as a source that can come to an end, believe that you have an abundance of it. This is an example of an Abundance Mindset, which is a much better mindset to be in as opposed to a Scarcity Mindset, thinking that you don't have enough willpower and that your willpower will run out.

Taking Baby Steps

As I mentioned earlier in this chapter, breaking your bigger goal into smaller goals that will bring you closer to your end goal is extremely beneficial for several reasons. One of the reasons that we have yet to explore is how it will help you to be more positive in your thinking and your self-motivation. If you are trying to accomplish one massive goal all at once, you are likely to become overwhelmed and to become discouraged. If you begin by focusing on just one small thing consistently, you will be actively showing yourself that you are capable of making changes in your life. You will prove to yourself that you are strong and dedicated, which will then motivate you to continue in your journey and continue achieving your smaller goals on the way to your bigger ones. It is then that you can add the next piece, and continue on in this way until you have reached your bigger end goal. Over time, your motivation and confidence will continue to grow as you will continue to show yourself proof that it is beginning to work!

Using Visualization

The technique of visualization is extremely effective when a person is learning new skills. This is because the brain is activated during visualization in the same manner as when someone is physically performing that action or that skill.

You can use visualization to learn and master any skill of your liking, but in this case, we will be learning about how to use visualization to improve upon the skill of assertiveness.

Whenever you are feeling stressed or overwhelmed, visualization can be a great way to help you build a plan that allows you to take proactive action and to stay centered toward achieving your goals.

The most important thing is to try to utilize all your senses when using the technique of visualization.

Here are five simple steps to teach you how to begin using visualization properly:

1. Pick a skill that is of interest to you

    In this case, assertiveness.

2. Identify what your real-world proficiency level is in this skill

    You can use the guide in chapter three to determine this.

3. Visualize yourself doing this skill using all five of your senses in as much detail as possible.

    For example, imagine a situation where you wish you were more assertive. Then, imagine how this situation would play out if you were your ideal level of assertiveness. Visualize what you would be hearing, touching or feeling, smelling, seeing, etc. to make this situation feel as real as possible.

4. Do this visualization for 11 days at 20 minutes per day.

   By practicing this over and over again, your brain will become more and more used to being assertive, and it will make it much easier for you to do this in real-life scenarios.

5. Try this skill in reality and keep track of your levels of improvement over time. Continue practicing your visualization

while also practicing this skill in real life if you are not yet satisfied with the level of assertiveness you have reached.

This visualization technique is most effective when practiced at the end of the day, so you can use it to begin planning the steps that you want to take toward achieving your goals the next day.

You don't have to be too strict with this, as you can also choose to use this technique throughout your day whenever you have a few minutes of free time, or when you feel like you need to get in touch with your inner self, your goals, and your vision.

Below are some other simple ways that you can practice visualization if you have less time to devote to it and you wish to benefit from the results more quickly and simply;

1. Calm yourself down and make sure that you are feeling relaxed. Sit down as it will help you get some rest from whatever you were doing before.
2. Close your eyes and start to visualize, specifically the things that you are looking to accomplish for the rest of your day and tomorrow.

   In our case, this would be practicing more assertiveness in your life. Visualize every action that you need to take in specific detail and then ask yourself the following questions:

   a. How do I want to feel?
   b. What do I want?

c. How will I interact with others?
d. What specific actions do I want to take?
e. How will I overcome obstacles?
f. What obstacles will I potentially face?
g. What do I want to achieve?

3. In addition, practice the following scenarios to help you feel confident and prepared to face anything that may come your way.

    a) Imagine a time when you felt extremely confident
    b) Imagine a time when you felt extremely assertive
    c) Imagine a time when you had a high level of self-esteem

The reality here is that people are not able to predict all the things that might happen to them. When events happen unexpectedly, they can often ruin any plans that have been put in place. For example, you will likely not be able to anticipate a situation that will require you to be assertive before it happens.

However, good planning isn't about planning around all possible obstacles; instead, it is more about adapting to the challenges that life gives you.

You must affirm yourself at the end of your visualization, using *affirmations*. Affirmations are, by definition, something that is spoken or written, which states something to be true. More specifically, affirmations are the valuable and uplifting assurances that we tell ourselves. They are words or phrases that we use to state something about ourselves or our lives to be true.

One great example of an affirmation that you can use in this situation is the following;
"I confidently take control of a situation when needed."

By giving yourself an affirmation, you are maintaining an open mind, no matter what will come your way next. There are endless possibilities for what life has in store for you, so it is important to remember that you cannot control every possible outcome. This will help you feel more prepared and comfortable with making changes when unexpected things happen to you.

Once you do this and make a habit of doing this,

you will begin to prepare yourself to effectively handle any situation that may require you to be assertive in your life.

A Note on Using Visualization

Using the technique of visualization for setting goals brings a lot of value, but this technique does come with one major drawback.

The most popular form of visualization involves the visualization of goals. Many people have used visualization to imagine themselves achieving their goals. However, this technique may not have worked for them because of one critical flaw.

This flaw is that when people are visualizing their goals, they often remain focused only on their end goal. They imagine their flashy and exciting end goal, without visualizing all of the hard work that will be required to achieve the smaller goals along the way to the end goal. By visualizing only your end goal, you may come out of visualization, feeling inspired and excited to achieve that end goal. Still, without looking at the steps that you must take along the way to get there, this motivation and inspiration will be extremely short-lived. The next time you face an obstacle, your excitement and drive will immediately dissipate as you realize that the path to your goal is not as simple or as exciting as it seemed during your visualization.

When this happens, people need to visualize their goals all over again in order to create more motivation for themselves. However, because nothing happens after every visualization, their motivation stays stagnant and does not grow, and therefore, their hunger for achieving that goal starts to fade. Every time a person hits an obstacle, and they try the process of visualization again, their motivation becomes weaker every time, and as time goes on, they begin to lose energy as well.

What they are doing incorrectly is that they are not visualizing their goals in the most effective manner possible. They only see the destination, but they don't understand that achieving a goal requires much more than just the final destination. The journey of achieving a goal is full of wins and losses, highs and lows, and a journey that is jam-packed with ups and downs. Because of this, there are additional things that a person must also include in their visualization to see the most success possible.

When a person visualizes their end goal, it is very effective in creating that desire and hunger. However, the proper way to use visualization is to only spend 10 percent of your time visualizing the end goal and spending the leftover 90% of the time visualizing the 'how' behind achieving your goals.

For example, if your goal is to reach a level of assertiveness where you can approach your boss and ask for a raise, visualizing this scenario will not lead you to wake up the next day, having reached that level of assertiveness. Instead, you must visualize the steps that you will take along the way. This may include visualizing the following scenarios:

1. Reaching a level of assertiveness that allows you to speak up about your

thoughts and opinions in conversation with co-workers.
2. Being assertive enough to say no to a friend.
3. Being assertive enough to challenge a coworker on something you disagree with.
4. Being assertive enough to speak to your boss one on one about your performance.
5. Asking your boss for a raise.

In some ways, it's similar to the form of visualization planning that we just discussed. A person's end goal creates the inspiration that they need long term, but the actual journey itself helps a person stay motivated in the short term. If you are trying to maximize the time that you spend on achieving small goals to get to your end goal, you must visualize those as well, just like you can see above in the five steps of visualization toward a final, end goal.

Below I have outlined an additional five steps that will allow you to practice this type of visualization if you need a little bit of extra guidance. If you do not have much experience with visualization, try this method instead until you get more comfortable.

1. Get yourself to a quiet place and sit down and shut your eyes. Start to imagine what your end goal will look like. Imagine yourself experiencing and living this goal using all five of your senses.
2. Slowly begin to take steps back from your end goal and imagine the process that was in place that you took to achieve

your end goal. Imagine yourself overcoming all of the problems and obstacles that you had to face. Keep visualizing every single step until you find yourself back into your present moment.

3. Move forward in time now and visualize how you took advantage of opportunities and the happy coincidences that aided you in overcoming any barriers. Try to see as clearly as possible how things unfolded for you.

4. At the end of your visualization, take a few moments to send your future self some positive energy for their journey.

When you exit the visualization, immediately detach yourself emotionally from the outcome of your goal. One thing that can hold you back is if you are having an emotional attachment to a specific result. Instead, try to stay open-minded and be flexible for the journey ahead.

How to Reprogram Your Mind to Be More Assertive

To reprogram your mind to be more assertive, there are a few different areas that you will need to begin working on. Over the next few chapters, we are going to examine these items and how you can begin to work on them in your own life. The first area is your self-confidence.

What Is Self-Confidence?

Although self-confidence sounds very similar to self-esteem, it is quite different. The dictionary definition is "a feeling of trust in one's abilities, qualities, and judgment." Self-confidence is more focused on the way you perform and how that gives you the confidence to keep going. When you are more confident in your abilities and performances, you tend to end up happier due to your successes. When you are feeling good about your capabilities, the more motivated and inspired you are to take action and hit your goals. Self-confidence tends to focus on past performances, which then creates momentum to better future performance.

The meaning of self-confidence can be a difficult one to wrap your head around. Here are a few examples of what self-confidence means:

- Being able to value yourself for who you are despite the mistakes you make, the type of work you do, and the type of work you don't do.

- Feeling good about yourself, and still feeling valuable despite imperfections.
- Being brave enough to stand up for yourself. This includes being assertive.
- Knowing that you are deserving of other people's respect and friendship.
- Accepting and knowing all of yourself, including both your strengths and weaknesses.

To take this one step further, it is also helpful to understand what self-confidence is <u>NOT</u>. Here are a few examples of what self-confidence isn't:

- Believing that you are perfect or believing that you should be perfect.
- Holding yourself accountable to unrealistic standards and expectations.

- Striving to live a life that is free of any struggle, pain, and problems.
- Being selfish and only caring about your own needs' and goals.'

The Value of Stepping Out of Your Comfort Zone

In this section, we are going to look at the comfort zone. Your comfort zone is a term used to describe the places, activities, objects, people, and everything else that you feel very comfortable with. Some people are afraid of change and choose to stay in their comfort zone, saying no to things that fall outside of it, and some people enjoy stepping out and allowing themselves to continuously evolve and grow.

Fear is the number one factor that keeps people

inside their comfort zones. As a result, fear can hold you back from experiencing growth in your life. As humans, growth is vital to our development and our interest in life. We are meant to grow and change as we get older, but fear can inhibit this growth. Our minds work in much the same way as our muscles. If we challenge ourselves by exposing ourselves to new situations or experiences, our minds will expand. As this happens, we can keep exposing ourselves to new situations, and our comfort zone will expand along with our minds. The things that we deem new and scary will no longer be new and scary after this, and they will instead become included in your mind as things that we deem safe and comfortable.

By keeping yourself within your comfort zone, you are holding yourself back from the possibility of many new things that could significantly add to your life, including opportunities for mental growth and new challenges. This is true whether you are currently fulfilled in your life or not.

How Stepping Out of Your Comfort Zone Relates to Self-Confidence

Fear can be related to low self-confidence because of a lack of trust in yourself and your ability to handle new situations. If you are not confident in yourself, you likely are not confident in your abilities, especially when it comes to coping with new situations or situations of conflict. We all have to deal with different things on a daily basis, and putting ourselves in new and uncomfortable situations is one of these things that we have to cope with and overcome. When we have a low level of self-confidence, we do not believe that we are equipped to deal with things adequately, and this relates back to fear. Fear of being unable to cope, fear of looking silly in front of new people, or fear of having a mental breakdown, can all come with having low self-esteem.

When we have high self-esteem, we have confidence in our decision-making abilities and our ability to adapt to new and uncomfortable situations. We can approach unique circumstances in which we may feel some fear with confidence that we will be able to get through it, and maybe even learn something through the experience. We do not let the fear overpower us, and we do not let it hold us back from saying yes to new things that may scare us.

If we have a low level of self-esteem, we will likely think that we will be seen as someone who is less-than or who is unworthy. This can cause us to be overtaken by fear because we are afraid that we will be rejected by new people or in new situations. Take a first date, for example, where we would have to go outside of our comfort zone by meeting someone new, spending time getting to know them, and hoping that they will enjoy this experience with us. For someone who has low self-esteem, they will expect that the person will not like them, that they will not enjoy the date, and that they will be rejected at the end of the date. This causes fear, and this fear may even prevent the person from going on a date in the first place. In this way, self-esteem and fear are closely related.

For someone with high self-esteem, on the other hand, they will feel as though anyone would like them and that if someone didn't agree to go on a second date that it must be something about that person and not themselves. A person with high self-esteem has confidence in their personality, in the way they conduct themselves and in their appearance. They may be nervous for a first date, but they will not be fearful of the person rejecting them as they feel deep down that they are enough themselves without needing validation from anyone else.

Fear comes into play when a person with low self-confidence or low self-esteem is faced with experiences or situations that they may feel challenged in. They do not have the confidence to think about these feelings of fear and be confident that they are able to overcome them. They would need to think about how they are a capable person who has overcome many other scary things in the past, which would give them the confidence boost they need in that moment. The fear will usually prevent them from going forward into these types of situations or experiences when they have the choice, as they are so focused on all of the things that could possibly go wrong if they agree to put themselves out there.

Tips to Build Self-Confidence

- Try to think and remember qualities that other people say you excel in. Even if you do not believe it entirely, this is a step in the right direction.

- Try to stop the negative chatter in your brain. Start to think of ways to reverse those statements.
- If you are having negative thoughts, ask yourself if you would say those things to a friend? If not, stop saying those statements to yourself.
- Make a list of strengths that you have. Try to think about what you would say about yourself during a job interview. Add those to your list.

How to Reprogram Your Mind to Be More Confident

Being able to accept your personal level of self-confidence is important. Don't judge yourself. Your confidence was built and developed by external factors in your childhood. You had no way of controlling those factors back then, but you do have a way of rebuilding it to a healthy level today. Put all the negative thoughts you may have about yourself aside and dive into this step by step guide.

Below, you can find an exercise that will help you to begin building your confidence level, which will, in turn, help you to become more assertive, as they go hand in hand. Before you start, ensure that you get into a quiet place and take time to be alone with yourself so that you can reach a deep level of self-reflection.

1. Positive You

Begin to think of a few of your positive qualities, and a quick description of what a *"positive you"* looks like.

For Example, I am hardworking, generous, and

friendly. A positive me looks like someone who is always helping others and meeting new people. I work hard in life to achieve goals that I can then use to help others. I don't shy away from challenges, and I am not afraid to ask for help.

2. Write Down Your Positive Traits

To be able to start acknowledging your good traits, you need to write them down so you don't forget.

Ignore any negative thoughts of self-evaluation passing through your mind. These negative thoughts will serve to minimize your successes and positive qualities. Remember that this is a bad habit that may come up when you are doing this exercise. When this happens, simply acknowledge it and let it pass, then move on back to the practice at hand. If those negative evaluations of yourself are being stubborn and won't go away, try writing them down. Sometimes writing them down and reading them to yourself will help you recognize how unfair those evaluations are.

Now, you are ready to begin recording your positive qualities. The premise here is to make a list of all the positive attributes you have. You can include all your good personality traits, achievements, strengths, and talents.

Before you start, here are a couple of tips to keep in mind:

1. When you are doing this exercise, make sure that you schedule a time in your day to commit to doing the task. Don't do it

when you are on the go or multitasking while you are watching TV. Instead, give it the time and undivided attention it deserves.

2. Remember to physically write down your positive attributes on a sheet of paper or in your notebook. Don't just make a mental note of it or write it on scrap pieces of paper. This way, you won't lose your work when you want to refer back to it.

3. You can write as many positive attributes as you can think of. There is never "too many." Brainstorm as many as you can possibly think of. You can also add to it over the course of a few days until you've got a nice long list.

4. If you are feeling stuck, get help from a family member or friend, someone that is

supporting you throughout your journey. Don't choose someone who you think may be a negative contributor. Other people may suggest some positive traits about you that you have yet to see in yourself.

5. Watch out for the negative self-evaluations as you do this exercise. People naturally tend to remember more negative things about themselves than positives. Keep in mind that these positive traits don't have to be expressed 100% of the time or be undeniably perfect. For instance, if you wrote down "hardworking" as your positive trait, don't think to yourself that you can't write that down because you played hooky once and took a sick day because you were hungover. Be fair to yourself.

6. Be sure to re-read the things that you have written in this worksheet or notebook. Don't just do this exercise and never look back on it again. It is imperative to re-read your work and reflect on what you have written frequently. Let all these positive attributes build up and sink into your mind.

If you find yourself getting stuck, feel free to use the following questions to help you:

- What do I like about myself?
- What are some positive characteristics that I have?
- What achievements have I had so far?
- What are some challenges that I have overcome?

- What are some skills that I have?
- What are some positive things that other people have said about me?
- What are some traits that I like in other people that I also have?
- If someone has the same attributes as me, would I like them?
- What qualities do I think are bad? Do I have any of those bad qualities?

To help you out a bit more in identifying your positive characteristics, I have provided a list of examples;

Organized	Considerate	Strong	Reliable
Artistic	Health Conscious	Avid Reader	Resourceful
Appreciative	Good Listener	Good-humored	Friendly
Well-traveled	Creative	Adventurous	Politically Conscious
Praise Others	Diligent	Responsible	Fun
Animal Lover	Active	Charitable	Animal Lover
Loved	Cultured	Good Cook	Determined
Helpful	Outdoors Person	House Proud	A Good Friend

Chapter 6 Summary

This chapter was chock full of information, including how to get in touch with your vision for yourself and how you can use this to help you set goals. We also looked at how you can reprogram your mind to be more confident and more assertive. We then looked at the importance of self-confidence and how you can begin to develop your own.

Personal Development Mastery

Chapter 7: How to Be More Assertive

In this chapter, we are going to look at some specific ways that you can work on your assertiveness.

Tips to Be More Assertive

Since we looked at the close relationship between a person's self-esteem and their level of assertiveness, we are going to look at how you can improve your self-esteem, which will, in turn, help you to be more assertive.

What is the meaning of self-esteem? This is a term that is used frequently, but most people don't know the true definition behind it. The dictionary example of self-esteem is "confidence in one's own worth or abilities." It is also commonly referred to as self-worth or self-respect. Self-esteem is an essential part of success. Don't get confused by thinking that having lots of self-esteem will get you to success faster. You need to have a balanced and healthy self-esteem for it to produce results for you.

Typically, people with low self-esteem fall into destructive behavior or depression. It can lead people to make bad choices or end up in abusive relationships. However, having an overwhelming self-esteem leads to narcissistic personality disorder. That's no good either. We will be exploring in more detail the ranges of self-esteem and how to identify where you are on the spectrum and also the right level of self-esteem for developing your assertiveness.

In this day and age, you have to constantly be reminding yourself of things that you have achieved, no matter how little or large. You have to continuously work on your self-esteem and other similar traits that go with it to be able to live a healthy life. Improving your self-esteem will change you by helping you to make the best decisions you can for yourself. It will also help you to feel great in your own skin. This will allow you to begin standing up for what you believe in, which requires assertiveness. This is yet another example of how self-esteem and assertiveness are inextricably linked.

Before we continue talking about self-esteem and how to improve it, let's talk about the main differences between self-esteem and self-confidence. To refresh our memory, self-esteem refers to the way you feel about yourself and how much self-love you have. Self-esteem is developed from experiences and situations throughout your life and has shaped the way you view yourself today. Self-confidence is how you feel about your abilities, and it can be different based on the situation. An example would be, I have a healthy level of self-esteem, but I have low confidence when it comes to solving math equations.

As mentioned earlier, when you are showing yourself love, your self-esteem increases and gives you more confidence. When you start to become confident in different areas of your life, you will begin to improve your overall self-esteem. Luckily, these two concepts work hand in hand so you can improve your self-esteem and self-confidence at the same time.

Now, what are some similarities with self-confidence and self-esteem? The main trait that they both share is the ability to believe in yourself. The problem here is that if somebody grew up in an environment where they were not valued, it will be difficult for them to develop the ability to believe in themselves. If they do not feel valued, they will have lower self-esteem. If they have lower self-esteem, they will certainly not be able to believe in themselves. If they don't believe in themselves, then they will for sure lack self-confidence.

To summarize, self-esteem is developed through events that have happened to you over the course of your life. Self-confidence is your ability to value yourself and the things that you do. Together, they form a partnership within you and plays a significant role in determining how you feel about yourself, your overall confidence level, and your assertiveness level.

Strategies for Being More Assertive

In this section, we are going to look at some tangible strategies that you can use to begin being more assertive. By this point in the book, you fully understand how being more assertive can benefit you, so now we will look at how you can begin to do the work involved in actually becoming more assertive.

Conflict is not an inherently negative or violent thing. It does not have to lead to the breakdown of relationships of any kind or yelling and screaming. It does not have to involve a dominant party and a submissive party or an expresser and a listener. Conflict can be seen in a positive way; in that it can help you to voice your thoughts and speak the truth. Conflict can actually serve to benefit relationships, as it challenges people to speak up for themselves. By allowing yourself to clearly and calmly express your thoughts and feelings, you allow yourself to be heard and seen and speak your truth, which is a valuable and important skill.

When using assertive communication, you are required to look deep within yourself to examine your feelings and your values. What this does is hold every person accountable for what they are actually feeling, instead of having everyone cover up what they are feeling with anger and aggression.

When you use assertive communication, you get used to being able to express your feelings in an articulate and clear manner, which helps in conflict resolution because everyone is then aware of what you need and what you are not getting. This makes the conflict resolution process much simpler as there is no guesswork involved. Sometimes, when there is a conflict you must try to discern what the other person needs or wants in order to resolve the conflict, but this is quite difficult because only the person themselves can know this. If they express it to you in simple and clear terms, you don't have to spend the time trying to figure out what it is they need and can instead skip right to the point of resolution. This greatly reduces the chances of miscommunications or misunderstandings, which can also be a cause of conflicts getting blown out of proportion or feelings of built-up resentment. For this reason, using assertive communication will help you to get what you need and express it to others.

This type of conflict resolution is not only for co-workers, friends, and family, but can also be useful in situations where there is a conflict between total strangers, or when mediation is required between two people who are in conflict. If you understand how to use assertive communication, you can employ it in these situations with a variety of people, but the common thread is that it leads to peaceful dialogue and easier conflict resolution. It can help to open lines of communication among people who would not otherwise have peaceful dialogue and creates an understanding between them. It is a powerful tool for any situation that you face.

Verbal Strategies

The way that we communicate verbally shows others that we are willing and able to communicate in an assertive way, which also shows them that you are open and ready to resolve conflicts and address issues calmly and directly. In this section, we are going to look at a few strategies for communicating assertively so that you can ensure you are being heard and respected, and so that you can show others that you are making your needs a priority.

Setting Boundaries

Boundaries are a way for you to express the things that make you comfortable or uncomfortable, or what you would like to happen or not happen within your relationship. Setting and maintaining boundaries is an essential part of being assertive in your relationship and taking care of yourself within that relationship. You should not put your needs to the side just because you are in a relationship. Creating boundaries means that both people will have a better understanding of what type of relationship they have together and what each of you needs and expects from that relationship.

The Art of Saying "NO"

Saying no is something that poses a challenge to many people, especially those who struggle with assertiveness. One of the best ways to show others that you are confident and assertive is to practice the art of saying "No."

If you are a person who likes to please others, saying "no" will be an especially difficult challenge for you. However, it is important to remember that when expressing your needs and your feelings, there will come times when staying true to yourself involves saying "no."

For example, if someone asks you to do something that you are uncomfortable with, you have two choices- you can make yourself uncomfortable and say yes, or you can stick to your beliefs and your values and say no. As an assertive person, you will choose to say no in situations like this.

There is no easy way to get comfortable saying no, but as long as you remember why you are doing so, you will get more confident in doing so.

Using "I statements"

Using "I statements" is another great way to practice being more assertive verbally.

The primary difference with this technique and other methods of conflict resolution or problem-solving is that it aims to resolve a situation to the satisfaction of all parties without having to compromise. It ensures that you clearly state your opinion and your position, which will help you to find the resolution that satisfies you most.

It aims to promote understanding and compassion instead of hurting and using judgment that is usually a result of confrontation and an aggressive communication style. For example, if you said something like, "You are wrong!" The person will feel attacked and stop listening. If, instead, you said, "I feel that this is right." This opens up the dialogue and clearly states your opinion.

Assertive communication diffuses situations before they become heated or aggressive and even prevents conflicts altogether by having everyone express themselves. Situations are resolved well before anger has built up to the point of an outburst.

Another example of this kind of verbal communication is the following;

Instead of saying: "You woke me up last night, and it made me angry."

You would say: "I heard you talking on the phone at 3 am, waking up to the sound of you talking made me feel frustrated because I need sleep. Would you be willing to talk on the phone before midnight?"

In this example, the person recognizes their feelings and what needs this is associated with. From there, they have verbalized this need and are expressing it to the person who is involved in the situation.

This brings us to the next verbal strategy, which is the importance of expressing your feelings, opinions, and wants.

Expressing Your Feelings, Opinions and Wants is Important

When it comes to being assertive, you must express your feelings, your opinions, and your wants. This is the basis of being assertive and one of the main reasons why people spend time reading a book such as this. Therefore, one of the most essential verbal strategies for being more assertive is to remember that expressing yourself is necessary and vital. Below, you can see the best way to practice expressing yourself so that you are heard and well-received by the people you are interacting with.

When we approach a situation with a demand or in an aggressive way, the other person will often shut down emotionally, and the conversation cannot reach a resolution. This is because it results in both people feeling defensive and on guard at this point. If you use assertive communication to make a request or to address an issue in a very non-threatening way, the chances of coming to a resolution are much higher. This works in your favor.

While it may seem like this will be hard to remember in the moment, it will come more naturally the more you practice it. If you do forget and you are unsure of how you can communicate assertively, one helpful thing that you can do is remember what type of communication you do not want to use. As we have seen, you want to avoid passive, passive-aggressive or aggressive communication. Remembering what each of these types of communication is can help you to determine how *not* to communicate.

A few examples of what you do not want to resort to would include the following:
- Judgments
- Blaming
- Shaming

By remembering how you do not want to communicate, you will be sure to approach any situation civilly and diplomatically, which will be the best way to be heard and understood by others.

Address People by Name

Being assertive shows others that you are confident in yourself and your opinions. One way to show this to people is by addressing them by name.

By using people's names in conversation, it provides the following benefits;

- It shows them that you are confident in your ability to remember and correctly use their name

- You are speaking directly to them, thereby commanding their attention
- You are showing them that you are not simply speaking to whoever will listen, but you are addressing them in particular
- It shows them that you expect an answer

All of the above points show a person that you are confident and assertive in your position. One simple trick, such as inserting a person's name into your sentence, comes with many benefits. Try this the next time you want to come across as an assertive individual.

Nonverbal Strategies

We are now going to look at strategies for you to use to communicate assertively in a nonverbal way. This may seem like a difficult task, but I assure you, the body language you choose can make a big difference in whether people perceive you as assertive or passive. Your thoughts and feelings become communicated when they can be observed in the ways that people carry themselves, such as their body language cues, eye movements, the amount of eye contact they make, or their facial expressions. You can use this to your advantage to send messages of assertiveness to people you are interacting with. Body language, tone of voice, and how you deliver your message plays a huge role in people perceiving you as assertive, so here we are going to look at all of the contributing factors to showing confident body language. If you are perceived as confident, people will expect assertiveness from you. People who are natural-born leaders often exhibit confident body language, so we are going to use these types of people as examples.

Confident Body Language

So how exactly do we show our people that we are confident? This comes down to nonverbal communication. We can say as many times as we like that we are confident in what we are saying, but if our body language does not show this, we are not convincing. We are going to examine the body language of each part of a leader's body. It helps to imagine a leader you trust or imagine someone who you would want to be led by. Get a picture in your mind's eye before reading the next paragraph. For suggestions, maybe they are someone speaking in front of an office of people, perhaps a captain of a sport's team, perhaps a chef in a restaurant. This leader does not have to be famous, or of political status, all respected leaders share very similar body language. Now that we have this image in mind, we are going to examine it from head to toe. Confident nonverbal communication looks like the following:

The number one spot we are going to discuss is the arms and hands. Because leaders often speak to large groups of people or speak to people from a distance, the arms and hands are very important. From a distance, this will be what they can see if they cannot make out the face or if they are not within earshot.

A leader wants their arms and hands to demonstrate ease and comfort with what they are saying and what they stand for. If you have ever seen a leader speak in a video, but you could not hear the sound, even without knowing who they are, you can tell that they are a leader. This is because of their gestures and movements. Keeping your hands out and visible is a sign that you are confident and that you have nothing to hide.

As humans, we tend to feel insecure if we cannot see a person's hands, especially if that person is someone leading us. Keeping your hands out and visible for all to see shows that you are being transparent and are confident in what you are standing for. While keeping your hands out, it is important to notice what they're doing. If they are fidgeting with their hair or clothing or something on the table in front of them, they will appear nervous or anxious. If the leader seems nervous and anxious, the followers will not feel secure in their leadership skills. The arms play a critical role in this. If the arms are moving and gesturing along with what the person is saying, they appear to be enthused and passionate about what they are saying. This makes them appear to be really believing what they are saying, whereas if they are standing with their arms stiffly at their side, or if their arms are barely moving, it makes them seem rehearsed and like they are not invested in their own words.

Gestures that are in tune with the content of one's speech and that are not too aggressive or over the top are best. Too many gestures can also seem rehearsed, and as if the person is trying to overly engage people. There is a sweet spot right in the middle that feels natural and confident.

To follow the arms and hands, the next section we will examine is the stance and the feet. As mentioned earlier in chapter two, the feet are an often forgotten piece to the puzzle of body language. The feet should be firmly planted on the ground, facing forward and not shifting nervously. While you don't want to stand like a statue, you do not want to be pacing or moving them in a way that demonstrates nerves. Leaders take up space—both with their arm gestures and their feet. The stance is created by where the feet are placed. In a confident stance, the feet are wide enough that you are taking up space. If your feet are shoulder-width apart, this is an appropriate amount of space that is proportionate to your body size. Taking up space shows that you are secure in your position, that you are not trying to make yourself small to fit in anywhere, that you are unafraid to be seen.

As with stance, posture is a demonstrator of

how you feel about yourself and your position. A leader will stand with their shoulders back, their chest out, and open. This is another way to take up space. Your shoulders will take up space just as your feet will, and this demonstrates confidence in yourself. Hunching your shoulders, closing up your chest space and folding yourself down is an indicator that you are trying not to be noticed, or that you are not confident. Appearing too rigid and upright can make someone seem intimidating and overly uptight, so avoid being too rigid. A nice confident but comfortable posture includes the shoulders back and the hips semi-forward.

The posture of the head is important for demonstrating confidence as well. The chin should be upright, and the head should be facing forward. The head should be fairly stable when speaking or standing and even walking, as this is a natural demonstrator of confidence. Leaders avoid lowering their heads or moving it from side to side as they speak as this can make them appear frantic. A leader who appears frantic is not one that people will readily trust with their best interests.

Until now, we have discussed what a leader looks like from relatively far away. Body parts and actions that you would notice if you were standing at the back of the room. There are also, however, characteristics of confident body language that can be seen when close up. Leaders must remain confident even in more intimate settings, such as one-on-one discussions. We will begin with the eyes.

While leading, it is important that everyone

feels included and encompassed by the care of the leader. When making eye contact, slowly scan the room, attempting to make eye contact with many people rather than focusing on one or two at the front. Leaders keep their eyes up, showing attentiveness and readiness to answer a question or address a concern. They avoid choosing just one person to focus on and avoid staring at the floor or the ceiling, or at inanimate objects for too long.

The way that a leader holds their face says a lot about how they are feeling. While there are those small, quick expressions that are very hard to notice or avoid, most people will not notice these. People will notice the facial expression as they will be trying to get a sense of how the leader is feeling. Maintaining a neutral and relaxed facial expression will show that you are confident even in the face of a problem, that you are prepared to tackle anything. Avoid too much tension anywhere in the face and ensure that your mouth is neutral or in a light smile. By appearing unphased by problems that arise, people will feel confident in your abilities to take care of them and their concerns or problems, no matter what happens.

One attribute of a good leader not to be forgotten is their handshake. A firm and confident handshake can be a great demonstrator of confidence. Have you ever shaken someone's hand for the first time, and it was a limp, loose handshake? This probably gave you a lot of impressions of them that you may not have otherwise had. Keeping your handshake firm and tense enough shows the person that you are secure in yourself and confident in your abilities. It is also essential to make eye contact while shaking someone's hand.

Speech

The next factors worth mentioning are voice-related; however, they are still nonverbal forms of communication. The first is the tone of voice. Hearing someone's tone of voice is telling whether they are speaking a language you understand or not. By someone's tone of voice, we can determine what type of talking they are doing. When a leader is speaking, it is best if they are speaking in a calm tone, with inflection where needed.

An assertive person sounds calm and does not sound erratic in tone. They are also careful not to sound too relaxed in fear of coming across as completely unconcerned.

Speed is another factor of voice that must be taken into account. If someone is talking with great speed, they seem nervous and rushed, and this makes people feel uncomfortable. If someone is speaking too slowly, this can be insulting to the audience. The right speed is slow enough to be understood while pausing naturally where appropriate. It should feel natural enough that you can think while you are speaking.

The third and final factor of voice to be addressed is volume. Someone who speaks too quietly appears unsure and tends to leave the listeners frustrated. Someone who speaks too loudly does not leave their listeners feeling engaged and can cause people to stop listening out of discomfort. Speaking at a tone where the people furthest from you can hear and understand you without blasting the front row with sound waves is the ideal volume. This demonstrates confidence in the content of your speech as you are committed to having everyone in attendance hear what you are saying. This also avoids you having to repeat yourself, which can leave you feeling nervous and flustered and will lead you to lose your air of confidence for the rest of your speech.

Your Attire

The clothing a leader wears can vary greatly by culture and region, but in a general sense, the clothing choice must be of a professional nature. Professionals can look like a suit, a dress, or traditional clothing, whichever is most appropriate for the setting. The choice of clothing demonstrates respect for the environment that you are in and concern for your image. Included in this are your hair and hygiene. Someone who appears to put time and effort into their clothing, their appearance, and their personal maintenance will appear to be prepared to take care of matters for their cause. If someone turns up to lead and they are unkempt and unclean, they will give off the impression that they are not able to take care of matters because they cannot take care of themselves.

It is essential that you take care of your physical appearance. Look the part; dress like a winner.

What Does Effective Communication Look Like?

In this section, we are going to talk about what effective communication looks like. This will help you to analyze your own communication styles and determine whether they are working for you or if they are working against you. We are going to begin by looking at the types of body language cues that an effective communicator would use.

The way that we communicate and listen with different types of people can be very different depending on our relationship with them. The way that we demonstrate listening behavior is very different if we are listening to our boss speak than if we are listening to our friend.

While it is important to show our friends and

family that we are listening to them, we can do so with much less formality of body language. In a one on one meeting with a boss or a superior of some sort, it is important to show them respectful body language. We demonstrate to them that we are listening with eye contact and a few silent nods throughout. We avoid interruption and asking too many questions until they are finished speaking. We maintain good posture and sit relatively still to avoid making unnecessary distractions. We ensure not to gaze off for too long to avoid seeming uninterested and unprofessional. When it comes to listening to a friend or a peer, the body language of listening is much less formal. While we do not want to show that we are bored or ignoring them, we can sit or stand with a much less rigid posture. Leaning or slouching a little is acceptable and even welcomed to demonstrate a relaxed attitude. If we were to be too stiff and quiet, we might end up making them feel uncomfortable. We can laugh and agree verbally, and even ask questions at the appropriate time to show them that we are interested and engaged. This type of active participation in the conversation while listening is a demonstration of care and concern for the subject matter and the person delivering it, while in a professional setting, it is more important to demonstrate a respect for the subject matter and the person delivering it.

Tips to Be a More Effective Communicator

- Pay attention to your body language cues
- Pay attention to your verbal communication style

- Exhibit confidence when interacting with others
- Show effective listening
- Make eye contact

Listen Intently and Effectively

Until now, we have discussed all of the above examples of how you can become a more effective communicator. The final lesson to becoming an effective communicator is through active listening. Here, we are going to talk about what that is.

When it comes to communication, a large part of this is listening. Listening is another skill that allows a person to be an excellent communicator. Half of the expertise of communicating involves the ability to receive and interpret the communications of others.

Active listening is something that can help make you an effective listener and, therefore, an effective communicator. Active listening involves not just hearing what is being said to you but taking it in and trying to understand it as well. Many times, we will hear the person speaking to us, but we will not really be paying attention to what they are saying. Paying close attention helps us to understand the information being shared with us so we can process it and respond accordingly. This type of listening will help you to get the most out of your communications no matter who they are with.

The second thing to note when becoming a better listener is your intention. Many times, we will listen with the intent to respond. Instead of paying close attention to the person we are speaking to, we are looking for the end of their turn so that we can say what we want to say. We may also be thinking of what we want to say next for the entire duration that the other person is speaking. Instead, we want to listen with the intent to understand. Listening requires an open mind. If our mind is full of thoughts about how we will respond and what we will say next, then we are unable to really listen and process what we are hearing. We may even think that we are listening, but it may not be in the most effective way for good communication.

If we can actively listen with the intent to really hear and understand the other person, rather than with the intent to play our part in the conversation, we can develop a greater understanding of other people. We can also develop a greater understanding of what they are saying to us to decide then how we want to contribute to the conversation, as well as the best way to do so.

If you can put these two parts of listening into practice, it will take your communication skills from basic to advanced, since people enjoy the feeling that they are being heard and understood. This will help you to better communicate with them, no matter what the situation.

Exercises to Practice Assertiveness

Here are some small exercises that you can try to help build confidence on your path to becoming assertive:

1. Ask a friend to lend you a book or household item
2. Ask someone for a favor without using the word "sorry"
3. Ask a stranger for directions, a pen, or change for a dollar
4. Ask a store manager for a discount on an item you are interested in purchasing
5. In the middle of a conversation, ask the other person to provide more clarity on what was said
6. Give compliments to friends and strangers

Chapter 7 Summary

This chapter shared with you a variety of strategies for practicing your assertiveness, including verbal and nonverbal strategies.

Chapter 8: Being Assertive at Work

Learning how to be assertive is an important skill to have in life as it is commonly used and respected in the workplace. If you can be assertive at work, you will be able to feel confident knowing that you can handle any situation that presents itself to you throughout your workday.

The Benefits of Assertiveness at Work

Being assertive at work will allow you to

communicate with skill. It will enable you to effectively manage challenging situations, no matter what office politics and difficult personalities are at play in your work life.

If you find that you are suffering from the "Yes" syndrome, you may need to work on your self-esteem to help you recognize and respect your own needs and wants.

To begin, we will look at an example of assertiveness in the workplace. Imagine if your boss just asked you for the third time this month to do your co-worker's report because he has fallen behind schedule again and knows that you work more efficiently than him. A person with healthy self-esteem will be able to have an assertive response as such "This is the third time in a month that I have received extra work because John is behind schedule. I value being a team player, but I feel stressed when I am overwhelmed. What can we do to make sure this doesn't happen frequently?"

That is the correct way to respond in a situation like this because you have to be able to respect yourself and say, "enough is enough." Typically, in this situation, a person with low self-esteem will agree to the extra work and end up resenting their boss for it. They will end up draining themselves by doing extra work and blame other people, which will create bad relationships. By being able to let people know how you feel and what you need will give them the chance to understand your needs and, thus, adjust their actions accordingly.

The Relationship Between Workplace Stress and Assertiveness

The textbook definition of stress is the "feeling of pressure and/or worry." However, not a lot of people understand that the main determinant of the level of stress you are feeling is not only based on the actual circumstances of a situation but the person's perception of their situation.

Lack of assertiveness causes a person to be thrown into a vicious cycle where the person with low self-esteem accepts more work than they can handle due to not wanting to appear 'weak' or incapable. This then causes higher stress levels as they have bitten off more than they can chew. You may start to begin noticing the trends throughout regarding how different effects of self-esteem begin to relate to one another, and they all play a role in affecting how someone feels. It's like intersectionality, but for your self-esteem!

The Art of Being Assertive in the Workplace

Passive people are not often treated very well because they have a difficult time expressing themselves clearly enough to make their needs known by others. Aggressive people, on the other hand, are often able to get what they want, but in the process, they also tend to step on people, not caring whose feelings they hurt. In addition to this, they sometimes interact with people who will fight back, and this results in a destructive and negative interaction. This is true for people both in the workplace and outside of it, but when it comes to conducting yourself professionally in an environment such as your workplace, you must keep this in mind. If you are too passive, you risk being stepped on and forgotten, but if you are too aggressive, you risk looking unprofessional and volatile.

The happy medium is assertiveness. Being able to be assertive in the workplace ensures that your work is noticed and respected, but that you do not make yourself look unapproachable. Finding that happy medium is sometimes tricky, but it will make the difference between ensuring your success or your demise in your workplace.

How to Deal with Difficult or Narcissistic Bosses or Co-Workers

Narcissists often have a lot of likeability and charisma that compensate for their negative traits. When it comes to gaining success in the world, charisma is one of the most important qualities to have. It is what makes people interested in you as a person and fascinated with the things you say. People that have a salesman type of personality often find themselves gaining more opportunities and are more commonly found in leadership roles in their careers.

Most narcissists tend to be people who are a sucker for power. A narcissist's tendency to gain adoration from people fuel their ideas that they can accomplish anything if they want to. While somebody that lacks empathy can get themselves further in life, it often is a result of immoral behavior and is achieved through hurting people around them. Their constant techniques of manipulation and exploitation of other people create an environment that is toxic for everybody that has a relationship with this person. With time, narcissistic people tend to damage the closest people around them. If every single person in our society were driven by egotism and selfishness, our society would become very undesirable. This is why there has been a buzz around narcissism; many people are looking for ways to combat or escape the increase of narcissists in our society today.

While overly confident people can run into their own set of downfalls, people with just the right amount of confidence can find and create great opportunities for themselves, as they are well-received in society. This is where your assertiveness will come in. Dealing with a narcissistic co-worker or boss can be quite challenging, but with the right amount of confidence and your assertive communication style, you will be able to handle them appropriately. It is important to use your newfound assertiveness to gain respect from your boss by showing them your work and your efforts in an assertive but not an aggressive way.

How to Manage Staff Assertively

Leading people, especially staff in the workplace, is a skill that involves many components, but that can have limitless positive effects on your professional life, as well as your development as a professional person in general.

As with everything else in life, leading and communicating requires a delicate balance of having enough positive qualities (such as confidence and assertiveness) without having too much of the negative qualities (such as being over-confident or narcissistic). By ensuring that you remain at just the right level of confidence and assertiveness without being aggressive or narcissistic, you will be able to have your staff respect you and put in good work for you every day.

It is essential to be assertive and fair with the individual members of your team. By doing this, they will feel noticed and respected by you. When it comes time to give them feedback about their performance, try giving them feedback as well as praise within the same conversation. This will leave them feeling as though you care about them and notice their positive efforts and will also make them more receptive to hearing your feedback. Lastly, always remember to be an active listener to their comments and concerns.

Managing Customer Relationships Assertively

It may seem like a difficult task to manage your customer relationships in an assertive way, however, as long as you understand the difference between an assertive communication style and an aggressive one, you can maintain the relationships in both a respectful and a firm way. This will allow you to maintain good relations with your customers without having to be passive and have a "customer is always right" mentality. As long as you remember your assertive communication style, your customers will respect you while also realizing that you are not someone who can be pushed around or easily persuaded.

How to Ask for a Pay Raise

To see how assertiveness can benefit you in terms of getting a promotion or a pay raise, we will look at a case study.

There are two employees that perform the same role in a corporate office environment. One of them is confident and self-assured. He walks into the office with his head held high and is quite talkative. He has a good rapport with the majority of the workers in the office, and he maintains a positive work environment. When he takes a phone call, he can be heard throughout the office as he speaks at a high volume and with a deep voice. The other employee is an extremely hard worker. He is quiet and shy, but he gets to work on time each day, and he works silently with focus all day long. He has never taken a sick day in his two years at this company and often works through lunch. He has not had many one-on-one conversations with his boss as he works in a self-directed manner and does not need much guidance. Which of these two employees will get the promotion?

While the majority of people would like to believe that hard work demonstrates knowledge and skill, and this will show itself, the silent hard worker who lacks confidence more often than not goes unnoticed. While it is unfortunate, in most cases, we cannot focus all of our time on our work to show our bosses that we deserve the next promotion.

What our employers want to see is the ability to work a room to display our knowledge engagingly. They want to see leadership qualities. While the second worker silently devotes himself to his work, his boss is noticing the more confident and more demonstrative employee who makes a point to start conversations with him each morning and tell him the latest work-related knowledge he has gained. As uncomfortable as it may be, we must be able to make ourselves noticed. This involves using our body language to our benefit. If we seem reserved and shy, we will not be entrusted with representing the company's image at a conference, for example. The employee who demonstrates confident body language, including a confident tone of voice, will gain listeners over the employee who is quiet but knowledgeable. We must work on the balance of confidence and skill to progress to where we want to be.

When it comes to asking for a pay raise without the presence of a promotion, it is essential to promote your achievements assertively. Without being over-confident, share your accomplishments and try to quantify them. This will show your boss that you are deserving and that you will continue to put in good work. Then, in an assertive way, ask for what you deserve. Do not be apologetic about it, and remain confident as you do so. You deserve a raise, and your boss will see that too if you can ask them confidently and assertively.

Chapter 8 Summary

This chapter focused on assertiveness in the workplace including the benefits of it and how you can begin to make this a part of your work life.

Personal Development Mastery

Chapter 9: Assertiveness in Relationships

A person with a healthy level of self-esteem can identify when their needs are not being met or are not being prioritized. If they can recognize this, they can assertively let their partner know that it needs to change; otherwise, the relationship will have ongoing issues.

On the other hand, a person with low self-esteem cannot recognize what their needs are, let alone if they are being met. They also do not have the assertiveness skills needed to be able to tell their partner that things need to change.

People who suffer from low self-esteem will often think that they are not doing enough, or not doing something right, and that is why their partner is unhappy. There aren't enough times where this person stops to think, "What are my needs?" or "Are my needs being met?".

Different Kinds of Relationships

Parental Relationships

Having a healthy and respectful relationship as a set of two parents is important for the parents themselves, as well as for the children. By having a healthy marriage or partnership, the parents can thoughtfully and respectfully join forces to parent effectively and raise emotionally healthy children.

If you are a parent, you have taken the first step

in parenting your kids in the best way possible by reading this book. Now that you are aware of the importance of being assertive and not aggressive or passive when you parent. It is essential to continue reading to learn more about how you can begin to use it in your everyday life with your spouse and your children.

Friendship

There is not only one definition of what a friendship constitutes or doesn't constitute. However, these are the most common traits of friendship:

- Both people have a desire for regular contact with one another. Regular contact could be defined as once a year or once every two days.

- There is some degree of commitment, whether it's to the friendship itself or both people's well-being.
- There is mutual trust, compassion, and concern.
- These two people share common hobbies, interests, beliefs, and opinions.
- These two people share knowledge about one another's interests, lives, fears, or emotions.
- These two people both share feels of respect, love, appreciation, or admiration of each other.

The points above indicate to you that for a friendship to be healthy and respectful, both people should feel that there is trust, concern, an understanding of beliefs, respect, and so on. What this means is that for you to have and maintain a healthy and true friendship, you must be assertive when it comes to your beliefs, your needs, your interests, etc. This will allow your friend to respect and account for your wants and needs.

Romantic Relationships

Traditional romantic relationships are generally between a man and a woman. Although this structure is very outdated now, romantic relationships are modernly described as when two people consensually agree to be exclusively in a relationship together where passionate love is shared. For a romantic relationship to be healthy, there must be mutual love and trust shared. In a romantic relationship, both people share a deep caring for each other, and they have a genuine interest in their partner's needs being met. As you get to know your partner, you will continue to share your beliefs and values with them. Then, over time you must be assertive as you ensure that your needs are continuously being met.

The Importance of Being Assertive in Relationships

Not only does being assertive help you to feel more safe, secure, and honest in relationships, it also helps you identify when the relationship you are in is unhealthy. The concept is simple; if you have healthy self-esteem, you can recognize your wants and needs and place a priority on them. If you have low self-esteem, not only are you unable to identify your wants and needs, you are not able to place significance on them. An unhealthy relationship is described as "a relationship where one or more of the people involved exhibit behaviors that are not healthy and are not founded in mutual respect for the other person."

How to Be Assertive Without Being Aggressive

It is important to keep in mind that being assertive is different from being aggressive. Some people shy away from being assertive because they think that it is the same as aggression. Being assertive means being firm about what you need/want while being aggressive is more of a demand. Body language, tone of voice, and how you deliver your message plays a huge role in people perceiving your request as assertive or aggressive.

Benefits of Being Assertive in a Relationship

Showing yourself love commands love and respect from your partner

Have you ever heard the saying that you must learn to love yourself before you can love other people? Well, this holds very true when it comes to being assertive in romantic relationships. Scientific research has confirmed the link between healthy self-esteem and relationship satisfaction. At this point, we know that self-esteem affects how we think and feel about ourselves, but it also affects how much love we are able to receive. It also affects how we treat others in intimate relationships. A person's level of self-esteem before entering a relationship can foreshadow the level of relationship satisfaction between both partners.

Although happiness generally declines slowly over time in relationships, this isn't true when it comes to people who enter a relationship with healthy levels of self-esteem. It is proven that those who enter a relationship with low self-esteem have the steepest decline of happiness. Moreover, those relationships don't tend to last. Although communication, emotionality, and stress are all factors that affect the outcome of a relationship, a person's past experience and self-esteem affect how those issues are managed. Therefore, it affects the outcome the most out of everything.

Having healthy self-esteem in a relationship allows for deep intimacy and someone to help take care of you as well. Having healthy self-esteem will cause you not to have problems like anxiety, abandonment issues, and avoidant issues. Since you are fulfilled, and your own needs are met, you will be comfortable spending more or less time with your partner. You will understand that you need to fulfill your individual needs first before you can attend to others. You will be comfortable expressing your genuine feelings to your partner and be comfortable listening to their feelings as well. Jealousy will not even cross your mind as you have complete trust in yourself and your partner as they have done nothing to break it. This is why those who enter relationships when they have healthy self-esteem typically sees success. The saying holds true that you need to learn to love yourself before you can love anybody else.

Reduces your risk of staying in an unhealthy or abusive relationship

Being assertive in a relationship allows you to understand when your relationship is unhealthy and when it is time for you to leave, since you have a good understanding of your beliefs and values, and you are not afraid to speak up about them.

Tips for Being Assertive in a Relationship

A healthy relationship involves assertiveness on the part of both people. In this section, I will provide you with tips for being assertive in your relationship.

Speak Up

When a relationship is healthy, the people in the relationship are comfortable with talking about a problem rather than holding it in, which allows them to get what they need from the relationship. They can also comfortably expect their partner to do the same. Honest, open, and safe communication is vital when it comes to having a healthy relationship. The first step into building one is to make sure both people understand each other's needs and expectations.

Expect Respect

Being assertive involves expecting respect from your partner and letting them know when you are not feeling respected.

Set and Maintain Boundaries

As I mentioned earlier in this book, setting healthy boundaries is an essential verbal strategy for being assertive. This is especially true in a relationship.

Boundaries are a way for you to express the things that make you comfortable or uncomfortable, or what you would like to happen or not happen within your relationship. Creating boundaries together as a couple means that both people will have a better understanding of what type of relationship they have together and what each of you needs and expects from that relationship.

Healthy boundaries should not restrict the following:

- Participating in hobbies and activities that you enjoy without your partner.
- Going out with friends or other people without your partner.

- Not needing to share passwords to your social media, phone, or email.
- Respecting each other's individual needs and preferences.

<u>Chapter 9 Summary</u>

This chapter focused on being assertive in relationships, including how you can do so. This chapter focused on helping you see the value in being assertive in your relationships and how you can do so without putting stress on your relationship.

Chapter 10: Assertiveness for Women

As a woman in today's world, it is difficult to be assertive or confident without seeming threatening. This can pose a difficult problem for women, especially in their professional lives. In this final chapter, we are going to look at some women-specific topics related to assertiveness.

The Importance of Assertiveness for Women

In general, men tend to be more comfortable than women taking up space in the world. Many women are less comfortable spreading themselves out in spaces and will more often make themselves smaller to take up less space in the world. Men also tend to be bigger than women in their shoulders and their height, so they will naturally take up more space regardless. Men tend to sit with their legs spread wide while women usually sit with their legs crossed or their knees together. If a man has his chest and shoulders spread, he is not necessarily attempting to appear confident and dominant because he could naturally have a wider chest and shoulders. This will affect the way that people perceive men versus women and the way that they perceive their level of assertiveness and confidence. For this reason, women must approach assertiveness from a slightly different angle than men do.

Further, in a general sense, men tend to be more aggressive in their movements, where women tend to be gentler and softer. An example of this is when a man performs an aggressive move when giving a handshake; a woman giving a handshake will tend to do so in a much softer and lighter way.

Challenges Women Face When Being Assertive

Below are common challenges that women face when being assertive, as the challenges they face are often quite different from the challenges that men face when trying to be assertive.

Fear of Disconnection in Relationships

There's a huge fallacy that declares assertive women are mean, harsh, or rude. As a result, many women spend their lives trying to make others happy, often at the expense of their own mental and emotional health.

Despite this misconception, always remember that assertiveness is about being strong and firm, but also kind and compassionate. It takes courage to set boundaries; set them, even if it will disappoint someone.

How To Be Heard Without Being Deemed "Emotional"

Women are often told that they are "too much" or are perceived as emotional when they are expressing themselves. Expecting this will make it much less shocking if you find that you are being perceived in this way. To deal with this, ensure that you are speaking assertively, showing assertive body language and that you trust in yourself and your knowledge.

Questioning Themselves

Women often question themselves and their knowledge, especially when they are being challenged. It is important to stick to your plan and continue to be assertive. This will help you to see over time that being assertive does work and that you are entitled to be assertive and stick up for yourself and your beliefs. If you can do this, you will no longer question yourself.

Strategies for Women

Below are some strategies for women who are wondering how they can increase their level of assertiveness without seeming "too much."

Trust Yourself

Trusting in yourself is very important as a

woman who is trying to remain assertive. It is difficult to trust yourself in a world that is telling you that you are wrong, but you must remember everything that you have learned in this book and trust that you are on the right track.

Be Confident

We have talked at length in this book about increasing your self-confidence, and this is very important for women who are looking to improve their level of assertiveness.

Welcome Failure and Adversity and Plan to Overcome it

As you are beginning your journey to change, it is essential to recognize that you will likely face some obstacles. By accepting this fact before they arise, you will not be surprised, but instead, you will feel prepared. Before you begin, take some time to write in your journal about what some possible obstacles may be. Once you have done this, take some time to plan and decide how you will deal with them when they arise, so that they do not disrupt your progress or cause you to resort to old ways that are unhealthy. By setting yourself up for success in this way, you will be able to tackle any challenge without having your success jeopardized.

Be Open to Learning

Other women can be an excellent resource for you as you embark on this journey to assertiveness, as they can tell you about their own experiences and vice versa. Be open to learning from these women, as their personal experiences can serve as great teachers for you.

Chapter 10 Summary

This chapter provided you with information about assertiveness for women and how this may differ between genders. This information will allow women to benefit from being assertive while also being aware of the unique challenges they may face when doing so.

Conclusion

Now that you have reached the end of the book, you are probably wondering - What is next for me? The answer is to keep practicing all the different techniques and exercises throughout this book. Practicing them in your everyday life will help assertiveness to become a habit in your life, making it your go-to style of communication.

Remember, I can only provide you with the tools to work with. Staying disciplined and continuously working towards your goal is your one-way ticket to a more fulfilling and assertive life.

By practicing the techniques mentioned in this book, you will build self-esteem and self-confidence, and you will be a new and improved assertive individual in no time!

In addition to this, ensure that you maintain your growth mindset! Understanding what the growth mindset is, as well as the benefits that it will bring to your life will help you to feel empowered and hopeful as you begin your journey of improving the skill of assertiveness. If you struggle with your confidence and your level of assertiveness, understanding that these are both skills that can be learned and honed over time means that this will not remain something that you struggle with anymore, especially after having read this book!

ONE MORE THING...

If you enjoyed this book and found it helpful, I'd be very grateful if you'd post a short review on Amazon. Your support does make a difference, and I read all the reviews personally so I can get your feedback and make this book even better. I love hearing from my readers and I'd really appreciate if you left your honest feedback.

Thank you for reading!

Personal Development Mastery

Personal Development Mastery

How to be Charismatic, Develop Confidence, and Exude Leadership

The Miracle Formula for Magnetic Charisma, Defeating Anxiety, and Winning at Communication

Richard Banks

Personal Development Mastery

Introduction

Do you want to become the best version of yourself? Do you want to become memorable, appeal to people, and find personal and business success? Do you want to overcome shyness and insecurity and become more authentic and popular?

If you want all these things, it means that you have everything it takes to become a charismatic leader, and this book will show you exactly how to do that! How to be Charismatic, Develop Confidence, and Exude Leadership: The Miracle Formula for Magnetic Charisma, Defeating Anxiety, and Winning at Communication will help you get from where you are now to where you want to be by developing ten crucial leadership skills!

This book is for everyone looking to develop social skills, establish deep relationships, open themselves up to the world, and attract people with their bulletproof confidence and intoxicating charisma. Don't believe this can be you? Just wait!

This book will show you the exact techniques and give you the right tools to find the deeply hidden seed of charisma and grow it until it bursts and shines through you in a blinding, jaw-dropping aura that attracts people like moths are drawn to a flame.

How will this book do this for you? It's quite simple. This book will teach you all about charisma and magnetic appeal that you can start nurturing and growing today on any budget just by reaching deep down into the most beautiful depths of your inner being. This book will show you how to find and grab your positive values, strengths, and talents and make them your trademark.

Upon learning how to harvest the fruits of charisma, you'll learn how to develop social skills needed to extend your network of acquaintances, enrich your relationships, upscale your career, and influence people to get what you want. This book will show you how to become an active, engaged, and empathetic listener who makes a killer first impression and leaves people hungry for your presence.

To do this, you will find out how to get people to like you, and it will not be by putting on a mask. No! You will learn how to showcase your authentic self with the way you dress, speak, and shake hands so that everyone who meets you gets to know and love what they see. If you follow the instructions given in this book, you'll be able to show others the genuine, strong, and confident you. You will know how to appeal to people's hidden motivations and desires and connect with what you have in common.

Once you learn how to get people to like you, this book will show you how to form better and deeper relationships. You'll learn how to master the art of small talk to set the basis for deeper relationships and leverage these connections to give and take for the sake of mutual progress.

That's right! This book will show you how to become an altruistic, inspiring, and charismatic leader who wears their life's true purpose like one wears a suit and helps other people achieve their goals.

In this book, you will also find out how to become more assertive so that you can balance your feelings and attitude for more productive work and personal relationships. Aren't you tired of being shy and hiding in your cocoon? No more saying yes to things you don't want and doing things that step on your dignity and self-esteem just to please people! In this book, you will learn how to set healthy boundaries so that you can show people what they can and cannot do and what you are and aren't willing to tolerate. More importantly, you'll learn how to do this in a calm, respectful way—that is, respectful both to you and the people around you.

That's right! Assertiveness skills explained in this book will show you how to stand up for yourself without hostility and conflict. Isn't that amazing?

But how do you get there? How do you appeal to people to that extent if you're introverted and shy? What do you do if merely talking to people frightens you? Don't worry—you're covered!

This book will give you the basic knowledge for growing and nurturing true confidence and self-esteem based on your authentic personality and best traits. In this book, you'll learn how true confidence looks and how to start practicing it so that you know and understand that you're an infinitely worthy person who can rely on their talents and skills to advance in life. You will learn simple everyday techniques and tips to apply to feel better about yourself and truly believe in your own worth. But that's not all!

This book will tear the misconception that loving yourself means being selfish, and it will show you how to be respectful, truthful, and empathetic. Aside from learning how to become a leader, you will learn how to become a leader who gives and contributes to their group or organization. You will learn how to share ideas and feedback that build everyone up so that you and the people around you are successfully working toward a common goal.

This book will also show you how to use the best of your abilities to observe and read people, as well as use your appearance, performance, and body language to speak and spread your authentic message. Following the principles and instructions given in this book will help you trade the best of your strengths for respect and popularity with your friends, coworkers, and family. Simply put, this book will show you how to reach into the best you have and share it with the world, and then you will receive the sweet fruits of your charismatic labor.

Don't wait another minute! Your hidden potentials, core values, and infinite strengths are waiting to be discovered, grown, and plucked to bring you love, acceptance, and success you so deeply desire. With each minute that passes, your potentials are being wasted on self-defeating thoughts and self-sabotaging behaviors, and you are losing time and money on doing things for other people just because you're unable to say no!

Hurry up and start learning to make a great first impression. At the beginning of this book, you'll find out what you can do today so that people remember you and want to connect with you. Aren't you excited to lead?

Get started now!

Personal Development Mastery

Chapter 1: Making First Impressions

Welcome to your manual for skyrocketing business and personal success by mastering the art of making first impressions. What if I told you that how you come across during the first 30 seconds of meeting new people affects nearly 85 percent of your business success? What if I told you that the person you like takes only a split second to decide whether they like you or not. Doesn't it sound scary? That's because it is! Just imagine. Out of thousands of hours spent learning and doing hard work to build your career, mornings and evenings spent working out to get yourself in shape, all the planning that goes into your career, or all the charity work you do to make the world a better place, those initial 30 seconds determine the majority of your success!

Why Are First Impressions Important?

If you still haven't freaked out, just wait. Remember the last time you made a new acquaintance. Maybe it was a bank clerk, a possible network connection, or your friend's friend who works for a major brand. It could even be your neighbor's coworker, who has a gorgeous son or daughter right about your age. What did these encounters look like? What did you say? How did you look? Were you clean and polished, or were you dressed in rags because you were cleaning your backyard?

How you carry yourself and act around other people determines your success regardless of your true skills, talents, and positive traits. Nailing that first impression can open many doors, point out shortcuts, and help you make long-term connections. But how do you do that? How do you make people remember you and want to talk to you in less than a minute? Lucky for you, you've come to the right place to get your answer.

Right before we get into the strategies for making an awesome first impression, let's briefly address why this is a challenge in the first place. When you're about to meet someone new, your fight-or-flight response gets triggered. Your unconscious brain evaluates whether or not you feel safe around the particular person, and it is particularly keen on detecting anything that's potentially threatening. If you look into the dynamic of first encounters, the truth is that it includes two or more people who instantly start deciding whether the new person seems safe to be around or they're to be avoided. Now, the way this works is that your unconscious mind detects the general appearance, body language, and other peculiarities regarding the other person and makes conclusions based on that. The same goes for those who evaluate you. The best way to make a great first impression is to send out more "green flags" than "red flags." This means to dress and behave in ways that help people feel safe and eliminate those behaviors that, unconsciously, signal danger.

How to Radiate Authentic Positivity for a Great First Impression

Having a positive attitude means allowing the best of you to shine through your attitude and conversations. However, this positivity needs to be genuine and not imposed (i.e., toxic positivity). It's important to remember to consistently work on how you see the world so that you're able to maintain a positive, optimistic outlook on a situation while acknowledging the present reality. A general rule might be that people prefer positive people. However, if your job is to market yourself as a grief consultant, to say that you should act punchy and upbeat would be wrong. In this situation, you should level your mindset to be empathetic with the people you talk to, but be positive-oriented in the way you send your messages and talk to them. When talking to people in a business setting or at a party, it would be appropriate to show your most confident, upbeat self. What do you do when that's inappropriate? Then you adjust to how you can make the situation better.

Toxic positivity, on the other hand, is present in people we perceive as disingenuous. These people make false claims and statements of not only their success but also what others can do. Their intentions are self-involved, and that's easy to notice. They can only fool those who are emotionally and mentally vulnerable—and even that is only temporary. So when speaking about positivity, keep in mind that I'm referring to a genuinely helpful, optimistic attitude in your appearance and mannerisms aimed at making everyone around you feel a bit better than they felt before they met you. At times, you will do this using jokes, and other times, it will be through consolation and the words of support.

7 Steps to Radiate positivity:

1. Stay in the moment.

To display this quality, make sure to leave all stresses and disruptions at home, and be focused entirely on the situation and people present. At the same time, learn not to allow other people to take away your cool. A lot of the time, it's impossible to shelter yourself from the influence of those we'd call "toxic" people. When you find yourself in a situation where the first impression matters, try not to react to other people's toxic or provocative behavior. If your reaction can't help or bring any kind of improvement, there's no reason to respond at all.

2. Tweak your appearance.

Whether we like it or not, we're all judged by first impressions. The way you come across the first couple of minutes may affect whether or not you'll get a job, a promotion, a date, a client, and so many other things. We're all taught we shouldn't care what people think about us, and it's indeed healthier not to obsess over it. However, it's essential to understand how the first couple of seconds may affect how others see you based on things like your facial expression, body language, clothes, and mannerisms. People around you evaluate your personality based on what they see on the surface. However, how will tweaking your appearance help make a great first impression? There are a couple of things you can do to present yourself in an authentic, genuine, and respectful manner.

Showcase respect. Want people to respect you? Start displaying respect first by being considerate of other people and their time. Particularly, be punctual and accountable. Whenever you're meeting someone new, make sure to arrive either early or on time. If you're late on your first appointment, you can expect to leave a bad first impression.

Mind your personal representation. Make sure that the way you dress for the occasion gives off the impression you want to create. Ideally, your outfit should be suitable for the situation. It needs to be a reflection of your unique, authentic personality and strategically chosen to send subtle cues and messages. Your outfit doesn't have to be a luxurious one, and you don't always have to be dressed elegantly to make the right impression. A suitable outfit will leave a memorable impression, and what better way to do that than showing up your unique, amazing style? However, it's important that you're clean and dressed appropriately, whether you're at work or in a networking event. In this sense, it's important to note that different occasions will require different outfits.

You wouldn't go to a wedding party in the same outfit you'd go to a business meeting. However, there are also many classic, timeless, chic outfits that, believe it or not, suit multiple different occasions. For example, the "little black dress" is a uniform design that you can wear in different situations from work to a wedding, depending on how you use accessories and style the outfit. For men, simple elegance, like plain black pants and blazer with a white or any neutral-color shirt, is also universally acceptable for the majority of different settings. If you're on a budget, think about getting a couple of new classic chic items you can wear throughout the entire day and still leave a great impression no matter where you show up.

Be authentic. Discovering your authenticity and unique behaviors helps you fit into any environment but still stay loyal to yourself. To be charismatic, you have to fit in at least a little bit. You're looking to belong but still stand out. Belonging, of course, stems from having certain connections to the group or a situation, whether it's a mutual goal or a problem to solve. Being your authentic self means having respect and integrity. It means respecting the integrity of the people you meet the same way you respect yourself. This will help you build up confidence and expand your social network.

3. Put on a smile.

Smiling and being in a good mood is memorable, and people always love being around those people who are cheerful and upbeat. A smile radiates warmth and confidence that will make people around you feel good as well. However, make sure not to smile too much and artificially. It could come across as insecure, fake, and creepy and give people the wrong idea about you.

4. Show confidence.

Confidence is one of the most attractive human qualities. It speaks more about you than can be said in your résumé. Showing confidence through your body language, eye contact, smile, and handshake makes people around you feel secure. While it's common for people to feel insecure when meeting other people, if your nervousness makes you uncomfortable and takes away from your experience, you can take some time before the meeting and work through your nervousness and anxiety. Another great way to appear confident when you're meeting someone for the first time is to set time aside to get appropriately ready, have everything you need in order, get there on time, and have a couple of minutes to spare to take a couple of deep breaths and calm down.

There's another way to cope with this kind of nervousness, and it is to accept it and be genuinely comfortable with it. Many people joke about their awkwardness and social mishaps, which help everyone feel more comfortable. There's nothing wrong with being shy. If you are shy, what you should aim for is to stop that shyness from keeping you from connecting with people.

5. Practice small talk.

Usually, during small talk, people exchange seemingly superficial questions and answers. Small talk may sound irrelevant, but it most certainly isn't. There are many subtleties we reveal about our personalities through small talk, and it is an excellent opportunity to connect with a person and take the conversation in a more significant direction. Every verbal exchange is a dynamic of giving and receiving information.

6. Grow your emotional intelligence.

What better way to master first impressions than to study emotional intelligence? You might think that your talents, qualities, and work results speak for themselves, but the reality couldn't be more different. People subconsciously make far more conclusions than one would care to admit. If you want to leave a good first impression, you should develop emotional intelligence skills to detect, interpret, and respond appropriately to your own and other people's feelings. These skills have developed remarkable communication abilities that help solve conflicts, negotiate, and work toward the common goal in almost every setting. People who notice that you possess sharp emotional intelligence will think of you as dependable and reliable.

But what is emotional intelligence? As the name suggests, it is the ability to be intelligent about feelings. More precisely, it means to have skills to look through superficial behaviors and detect people's feelings and intentions. To develop these skills, you first need to develop your own emotional awareness, which is the ability to understand how you truly feel. More importantly, developing emotional intelligence helps you see how your emotions guide and affect your motivations, decisions, and behavior. There are a couple of ways to nurture your emotional intelligence.

Practice self-reflection. Self-reflection is a method through which you evaluate how you think and feel and, more importantly, how that affects your actions. Before showing up to your meeting, take a moment or two to reflect on what you think and how you feel in these situations. This will help you match your attitude to the person you're speaking to or a situation you're in. If you're nervous and anxious, it's possible for your mindset to be inward-focused, and you lose the connection with the dynamic of the situation.

Level your energy. Learning how to adjust your energy to the situation and the person you talk to helps you connect and relate to them. With your emotional intelligence skills well developed, you will be able to adjust your body language and energy to the room. For example, a formal setting and a wedding party will require two different approaches to how you carry yourself.

Focus on the other person. Paying attention to what the other person is talking about and being a careful listener helps you connect and leave an impression. For this, it is also vital to remove any distractions and put away your phone to maintain natural, steady eye contact. To avoid coming across as uninterested, you shouldn't interrupt another person while they're speaking. Also, if you talk to another person while thinking about the next thing you're about to say, it can come across as rude and uninterested as well.

7. Focus on common interests.

Finding something that helps you relate to the person you're talking to helps find interesting topics for both of you to enjoy. This way, the other person will remember that they related to you in some way, particularly if the topic was fun and interesting. One of the best ways to find common interests with another person is to ask questions. However, pay attention not to come across as an interrogator. If another person is shy, they might feel uncomfortable being consistently asked questions.

Master the Art of Asking and Answering Questions

Common courtesy is to begin a conversation by asking some basic questions about the other person. Typically, in informal settings like meeting and job interviews, those higher on the ladder will initiate the conversation and ask questions, while the ones aiming to get a job or raise funds for their business will be the ones answering them. When answering common questions, it's important to remember to keep your answers medium length and open-ended. What does this mean?

You should never give one-word answers unless specifically told to do so. Answering questions like "Where you are from?" and "What do you do?" can be tricky for shy people, as they might give one-word answers and freeze the conversation. Instead, you should provide answers that say a little bit more about you and comment on what you like and appreciate about where you're from and what you do. You can also give a backstory of how you started working on a job you're currently at.

Aside from these common questions, questions that revolve around your work and career are quite common in job interviews and networking events. Here's how to answer some of the specific questions during job interviews:

"Why do you think you're the right person?" Whichever position you're applying for, the interviewer will want to know what drives you and makes you excited to do the job. Here, you should take the opportunity to speak about skills and experiences and how you can use them to contribute to the organization in that particular position.

"Why are you changing jobs?" Interviewers will want to know which circumstances led you to quit the current job

and look for another one. They will want to know all about your past work record and employment history, as well as why you left your previous job. It's imperative to give well-thought-out but genuine answers, or else you might leave a bad first impression.

You, too, have the right to ask questions during interviews. Here, you can take the opportunity to find out more about the job post they advertised. Asking questions about details that are important to you shows initiative, and it shows that you're interested in the entire organization and not just getting a job.

Ask about leadership and career development. Whether or not it will be appropriate to ask this question during a job interview depends on many factors, mainly on the work culture of the company. If you notice that the company values personal goals and leadership development, you can share your goals and find out how the position relates to your idea of personal growth. If you don't think this approach is right for the position you're applying for, you can show interest in senior management or other team members and ask how they obtained their positions and how long have they been with the company.

Summary

In this chapter, you learned that first impressions can make or break your chances of success all around. You learned that to make a great first impression, you must:

- Be considerate, present in the moment, and focused on the people around you
- Look and act confident, which you'll show with a proud, strong, tall posture
- Master the art of casual conversation
- Focus on talking about mutual-interest topics and goals
- Ask and answer open-ended questions that are interesting, strategic, appropriate, and engaging.

Now that you know how to make a great first impression, it's time to learn how to build and exude true confidence. In the next chapter, you'll find out not only how to look and act but also how to nurture the rock-solid confidence of a true leader.

Personal Development Mastery

Chapter 2: Confidence and Mindset

Confident people are universally attractive. They are easy to work with, trustworthy, and inspiring for others. Their inviting attitude attracts people around them. However, it's not always easy to remain confident in your abilities. This can be particularly difficult for those who are self-critical or those in an environment where other people put them down. Luckily, there are many things you can do to improve your self-confidence.

How to Build Rock-Solid Confidence

Self-confident people are able to trust their abilities and judgment and feel worthy while embracing their imperfections. They understand that no one is perfect. They're not chasing after perfectionism; instead, they accept their limitations as something natural and normal. Being self-confident also relates to self-efficacy, which is the ability to feel like we're competent to achieve goals and gain skills. This feeling helps up open up to the idea that we're able to do things if we put in enough effort, accounting for realistic obstacles and chances of failure.

Self-esteem, on the other hand, is a feeling or an acknowledgment that we have the right to be happy and appreciate ourselves regardless of what goes on in our lives. When people condition their self-esteem with exterior validation and proof of success, that means that they only allow themselves to feel good when the conditions for that are in place. Whenever a challenge arises, they start feeling bad about themselves and deny their right to happiness. As you can see, this isn't a great way to deal with challenges, isn't it? When you're making first impressions, people tend to notice these things about a person's character. It can cause mistrust in people, as they sense a person will lose their grip in situations that are stressful and challenging, which is not something most people want at work or in personal life.

A sense of self-esteem also links to caring too much about whether or not people around us approve what we do. While we're in very little control of whether or not someone will approve our actions, learning how to process criticism and rejection is valuable here (Klitch & Feldman, 1992). Low self-esteem may cause you to take negative feedback of any kind too personally and feel like it speaks about your personality when, in fact, it only reflects your actions.

As you can see, as opposed to a strong, confident appearance that instills trust, acting insecure and shy can make people see you as someone they don't necessarily want on their team or in their life, particularly if they were already hurt by someone else's insecurity. You may not be aware of this, but people who are led by their insecurities tend to make many mistakes at work and in personal relationships that can harm others (Griffin et al., 2007).

Actions that serve to save face or cover an error can make people feel invisible and insignificant. The same is true when you are too shy to express feelings and show another person you value them being in your life. On the surface, people call those who are insecure or shy, harmless and pleasant, while they unconsciously perceive them as a potential liability. At the very least, people don't tend to remember those who are timid and withdrawn.

How to Boost Confidence

Most people think that strengthening one's confidence means eliminating insecurities. You might think that if you simply address those issues that make you feel insecure, you will automatically become confident. While confronting personal fears and limitations does help reduce the impact of low confidence on your life, it doesn't heal the inner wound completely. The missing link in growing your self-esteem is the habit of strengthening it, much like the empathy muscle mentioned earlier.

Here are a couple of ways to develop confidence and self-esteem:

1. Face and challenge negative thoughts. Think about the reasons why you feel so bad about yourself, and find out which positive thoughts and ideas outweigh those negatives.

2. *Practice healthy self-care.* Feeling and looking bad won't help you feel more confident. To enhance your well-being, embrace diet improvements and exercise. Living a healthy lifestyle helps reduce stress and makes you feel better about yourself. Aside from exercising, setting aside enough time to relax each day also helps you reduce stress and tension.

3. *Be goal-oriented.* Take some time each day to think through your life goals. Think about the things you can achieve and write down your thoughts. Track your accomplishments as you complete goals, keep yourself motivated, and collect the evidence that will strengthen your confidence and self-esteem. Oftentimes, people with low self-esteem notice their failures but not their successes. For example, they stress more about the fact that they can't find a job in their field with a college degree instead of focusing on how proud they are for earning their degree and working another job until a better opportunity arises. By collecting evidence of your accomplishments, you'll focus more on the good things you've done instead of those you think prove your failure or lack of worth.

4. *Step out of your head.* There's nothing more nurturing for one's self-esteem as practicing love, care, and empathy for others. Research shows that there are actually health benefits or so-called "happy highs" in people who do charitable work (Deiner & Seligman, 2002). When you step out of your mental prison, where your thought process revolves around plans, ambitions, and insecurities, and forget about them for a little bit to help others, your brain switches to feeling happy and proud for having helped or cared for others around you.

Exercises That Help You Eliminate Self-Doubt

Do you doubt yourself when you're nervous or fear you'll say something wrong? Here are a couple of proven strategies to not allow self-doubt to get to you:

1. Stop negative thoughts. Never allow discouraging thoughts to spiral out of control. Understand that shyness and insecurity are natural and normal and that everyone experiences thoughts of insecurity. These thoughts have a physiological background, and you can't eliminate them. But you can stop yourself when you notice you're focusing on them and giving them too much of your time. When you're about to meet someone new, and you start thinking negative thoughts about yourself, just say "Stop."

2. Bring back encouraging memories. Be it the first time you successfully rode a bike or you jumped off a tall wall thinking your life is about to end only to land safely and without a scratch, recalling encouraging memories helps you remind yourself of your ability to succeed and overcome obstacles. Encouraging memories and experiences have the power to instantly relieve anxiety and bring back the smile on your face, making it easier to give a confident handshake and share eye contact that's reassuring for both you and the other person.

3. Get feedback. One of the great ways to overcome insecurity is to get frequent, unbiased feedback. It will help you be more aware of your strengths compared to weaknesses. Talking about your insecurities with friends and family will undoubtedly result in reassurance in how valuable you are to them, which will have a long-term empowering effect.

4. Stop comparing yourself to others. There is a correct way to estimate the quality and efficiency of your work, but comparing yourself to others isn't one of them. It's because you're comparing yourself against an exaggerated impression of how another person's life looks. You might admire someone's looks and career, but you don't know how much effort they put into these areas and whether or not they may lack some of the things you have.

5. Write a journal. We tend to forget positives and focus on negatives. It is a habit that's hard to shake for a 21st-century human. Mainly, this is because we are so hard on ourselves and aim for perfectionist goals. Create a habit of writing down at least one page in your journal each day, summing up at least three things you're proud of and three things you want to do differently in the future.

And that's it! These strategies will undoubtedly help you overcome that inherent insecurity and let your best self shine through.

How to Go from Nervous to Confident in Less Than Two Minutes

Building true confidence is a long-term venture. It's safe to say that, while you should be patient with improving your self-image and learning how to believe in your strength for months and years, you're going to need quick, effective strategies to act confidently in the meantime. Here's how to boost your confidence instantly for a killer first impression:

1. Stand tall. Straighten your back, keep your chin up, and pull your shoulders back. Make sure your hands are still. Your posture should be straight, chest open, with your head slightly tilted back. This way, you will open up your posture for communication and appear more approachable. As you start to look more confident, people will find it more interesting to interact with you.

2. Create new experiences. If your routines are constant and predictable, make sure to check out some new restaurants and coffee shops, or perhaps try out a new sport, or have a fun trip. New experiences help you change your environment a bit, which inspires creativity and appreciation of the things around you.

3. Focus on your talents. Doing new things does challenge

your fears and boosts confidence, but doing something you're good at strengthens your belief in yourself. Working on your talents and engaging in hobbies help you see what you're capable of. This enforces a positive self-image and enables you to think highly about yourself.

4. *Change perspective.* Questioning whether situations and events are truly as bad as they seem helps you question negative thinking patterns and overcome them gradually. Whenever you feel like you're failing or like you've embarrassed yourself, try to challenge these thoughts by asking yourself:

- "Is there a way to turn the situation around so that it works in your favor?"
- "Are there any hidden benefits to the situation you can focus on?"
- "Is there a better way to look at the situation?"
- "What lesson can I learn from this that will help me in the future?"

5. *Focus on your breathing.* Whenever you start feeling shy and insecure, your heart rate will increase, and your breathing will become shallow. Now, you're low on oxygen, which will only increase your anxiety. Instead, focus on taking three to five deep and even breaths. This will help you calm down and have more positive thoughts about yourself.

How to Solidify Confidence and Don't Clam Up in Social Gatherings

As you learn how to build rock-solid confidence, you shouldn't let shyness prevent you from attending and enjoying social gatherings. If you're shy or socially anxious, there are a couple of techniques you can use to feel more socially competent and be more present during social events.

Here are a couple of tips to be more confident during social events:

1. Get ready. Being self-conscious will ruin your mood, and one of the ways to prevent it is to be prepared. Make a list of what you want to do to get ready for your workday, a trip with friends, a party, or a meeting. Write down what your main purpose is, what you want to say and do, and, more importantly, how you'll plan your look. Think about what you'll wear and how to do your hairstyle. What are the self-maintenance items to cross off (e.g., shaving, getting a haircut, or visiting a cosmetician)? Feeling like you're all ready and polished will boost your confidence.

2. Focus outwards. Instead of focusing on what you think and how you feel, look at the room and notice a couple of things you like. Pay attention to the drinks and food, and think about the snacks you'd like to try out. Also, try observing other people. How do they look? What are they doing? What are their roles? What do you like about them? Thoughts like these help you stay focused on the exterior and forget about nervousness, at least temporarily.

3. Keep yourself busy. Being active, talking to other people, and smiling will help pass the time and feel better. The more you engage with other people, the more you'll forget about negative and anxious thoughts. If you ever start to feel anxious thoughts arising, shift your attention to other people, and ask more questions about them. This will make for a pleasant chat and help you overcome anxiety.

Positive Thinking and Positive Self-Talk

Positive self-talk can help you increase not only your performance but also how you feel about yourself overall. A negative self-image can sabotage all areas of life, from health to relationships and even work. On the other hand, a positive self-image can help you boost your shape, advance career, and introduce the right people into your life.

Positive self-talk serves to change your thinking patterns gradually and consciously. It revolves around catching yourself making an inaccurate, exaggerated negative statement or thought about yourself and examining and changing it. Here's how you can apply positive self-talk to improve confidence and boost self-image (Neck & Manz, 1992):

1. Identify negative self-talk. Conscious negative thoughts are easy to spot, but unconscious negative thoughts work differently. You don't register them, but they suddenly make you feel tense or afraid without any reason. More importantly, they reduce your drive and motivation. Whenever you suddenly feel down or you observe that you're now having self-defeating thoughts, analyze them. Ask yourself whether these thoughts are accurate or there's a chance they aren't.

2. Reframe negative self-talk. Once you've discovered a self-defeating thought pattern, try to tell a different story to yourself. Reword the same statements in a way that's positive, optimistic, and respectful of your personality. If you find it difficult, try reframing negative statements to make them more realistic. This eliminates negative exaggerations, which occur once catastrophic thinking skews your judgement.

3. Practice positive self-talk. Develop a routine of saying positive affirmations about yourself each day. These affirmations should be believable, or else they might trigger anxiety.

How to Improve Your Self-Image

What exactly can you do to improve your self-image? First things first—you need to identify your negative thoughts and review the reasons why you have a negative self-image.

Negative self-image manifests itself in four different self-sabotaging behaviors. First, it makes you personalize negative experiences and blame yourself for everything that goes wrong in your life. Second, this negative perspective gets unrealistically magnified. You're capable of ignoring all the positive aspects of a situation, and instead, focus only on the negatives. This thought process becomes habitual and unconscious, creating a self-sabotaging pattern that makes you look at yourself in a negative light. Third, you start expecting the worst. The more you focus on the negatives, the worse outcomes you start to expect, even if the catastrophic scenario opposes logic. Fourth, you start thinking in polarizing ways. Situations are either black or white without the possibility that there are positives in negative situations and other ways around.

Once you start recognizing your negative thinking patterns, you can move on to use the following strategies to improve your self-image gradually (Mayo et al., 2012):

1. Battle negative self-talk. Learning how to identify the negative things you think about yourself will help you start opposing them with rational evidence. Looking into what scares you the most about interactions will help you rationalize whether or not the scenario is realistic, and it will prepare you for the best possible outcome. As you mingle around and socialize, pay attention to when negative self-talk starts to arise. As soon as this happens, let yourself know that you are wrong and oppose these thoughts with realistic yet more optimistic ones.

2. Take yourself less seriously. Negative self-image sometimes manifests itself in some strange behaviors. Perhaps you exaggerate in your mind how serious a meeting will be and get ready to give a detailed presentation only to realize everyone else just came there to share a couple of important points and order a pizza. Try to see the humor in your negative experiences. Over time, this will help you dread catastrophic outcomes less.

3. Tune into positivity. People with negative self-image don't benefit from melancholic content. Choosing to watch, read, and listen to positive content may be the best solution in the long run (Berry & Hansen, 1996). Look around and discover the items, choices, and other influences in your life that spark negative feelings. You may like watching horror movies, but if you tend to become upset easily, perhaps you should choose a comedy over watching *Annabelle* tonight. Moreover, try wearing light-colored clothes instead of dark ones, or play some calming ambiance music instead of gothic rock.

Believe in Your Worth

Having a high sense of self-worth means having a profoundly positive opinion of yourself and carrying unshakable faith in your abilities. The challenging part here is that this faith needs to persist through challenges and endure whenever you fail. People who have a high level of self-worth feel like they deserve love, happiness, success, money, and all the wonderful things in life. Do you truly feel like that? Many of us are raised to think that we should have all these things, but we don't necessarily feel like we deserve them. This is the reason why we're plagued by anxiety, fear of failure, and many other self-imposed limitations that diminish confidence and productivity. How do we change this?

The answer is by making consistent, daily efforts to feel and think good about ourselves. Now, this is easier said than done. Luckily for you, there are many easy, reasonable steps you can take each day to nurture your sense of self-worth:

Step 1: Detect and identify how you think and feel about yourself. You can do this by thinking about or visualizing who you are when you take away all attachments to your physical life. This means imagining yourself without connections, possessions, accomplishments, and other material things. When you see yourself all alone, with nothing holding you back, what is it that's left? How would you feel knowing that all you have left is yourself? What do you possess that would be of real value? This is the part where you discover what you genuinely like and admire about yourself.

Step 2: Accept who you are. Most of us go by an ideal image of ourselves that doesn't always represent our true, authentic skills, desires, passions, and abilities. Now that you've discovered who you think you are and how you feel about yourself, it's time to accept it. There's a possibility you don't particularly appreciate what you've discovered. Perhaps you think your qualities are not enough. So what? The very act of acceptance means starting to feel and think positively about what you've discovered yourself to be. Even if your level of self-worth isn't at the desired level, still accept it and remember that from now on, you can only improve. The trick with acceptance is to push that deep, unconscious button and say, "This is it, and this is enough. I am enough." Just doing this will kickstart a chain of unconscious processes that will shift your mindset. Here, it's essential to understand that you're accepting yourself with all the positive and negative qualities because you have the right to have negative traits too. Everyone is at least a bit selfish, envious, lazy, or mean at times. That doesn't make you a bad person.

Step 3: Start loving yourself. Nurturing self-love needs to be done every single day and particularly when you feel like you're failing. You always, under all conditions, have the right to feel compassionate, generous, kind, and patient with yourself. But don't confuse this with accepting and condoning doing negative things. Many people deny love to themselves, thinking that if they accept and love their whole being unconditionally, they'll unleash some sort of selfish, destructive inner monster. That's not true. Quite the opposite, now that you're giving yourself unconditional and endless love, you will feel more aware of other people's needs and have abundant supplies of tolerance and generosity for everyone else. To nurture true self-love, don't forget to repeat encouraging mantras like "I love and value myself," "I accept and love myself unconditionally," and "I believe in my worth and competence."

After you've done this, it's time to start recognizing that you don't have to please others. Review and look into all the things you do just to fulfill other people's expectations. Many people feel that it is selfish not to please others, but it's not. Instead, you'll enter a stage of self-responsibility, where you realize that you and you alone are solely responsible for your life and well-being.

Summary

In this chapter, you learned that charisma, networking, and influence require building strong confidence, unshakeable self-esteem, and positive self-image.

To grow strong self-confidence, you have to challenge negative thoughts, practice healthy self-care, stay focused on your goals, and be in the present moment.

To eliminate self-doubt, you need to stop negative

thoughts, recall positive experiences, ask for feedback on your actions and performance, stop comparing yourself to others, and keep track of your thoughts and experiences by journaling.

To boost confidence instantly, stand straight and tall, meet different people and create new experiences, concentrate on your talents, change your perspective, and focus on your breathing to calm down and regain mental clarity.

Personal Development Mastery

Chapter 3: The Power of Listening and Remembering Names for Magnetic Charisma

A person's name is to him or her the sweetest and most important sound in any language.

—Dale Carnegie

Becoming charismatic starts with learning how to connect with other people. Charisma is a complex set of qualities that make a person attractive. It is an invisible quality that stems from one's inner traits rather than the exterior. Charisma is also an essential trait of all public figures or leaders, whether they're politicians, professors, or actors. It also revolves around the power of persuasion—the ability to motivate people into doing what you want. It is practiced using one's words, facial expressions, and body language. A charismatic appeal motivates and inspires others, so they become attached to the person they find inspiring. However, it's not a skill taught openly or directly. But how can you become more charismatic?

Why You Need Interpersonal Skills to Become Charismatic

The first step in becoming a charismatic leader is to develop your interpersonal or communication skills. These skills, while inborn, can be grown and developed. Personal charisma revolves around being genuinely interested in people and detaching from devices and inner negativity that might be present while you converse.

Another important yet intangible element of charisma is the art of influencing people to like you. But how do you do this when you're not able to affect what others think? The answer is by exploring and showcasing the utmost best of your personality and traits. When natural and authentic, charisma can last through years and even decades. When forced and inauthentic, it can become drained. To become truly charismatic, you'll have to exercise confidence skills and master the art of likeability, listening, and body language.

The five basic skills needed to become charismatic include authenticity, rapport building, listening skills, and confidence. In this chapter, we'll focus on those skills you need so that you can create deeper connections with people you talk to. Growing these skills will help you connect with an entire group of people. This happens as the charisma shines in your appearance—from your eyes to your body language:

1. Correct your posture. First, pay attention to your posture. Sit and stand straight with your chest open to display inner strength and openness. The two relate because people become closed, which they display by slouching when they feel weak. This means you need to keep an open body posture, which will make you more approachable. Also, make sure to pay attention to other people's body language. It shows who feels secure, confident, inviting and who needs empathy and encouragement.

2. Respect other people's personal space. Another important part of connecting with people is to respect other people's personal space. Make sure never to get too close or touch people while you're talking if you don't know them well. When talking to other people, try finding common ground even if your opinions don't agree. One of the great ways to show disagreement is to express your argument and then state that you can see how and why certain situations or events could lead the person to think and feel the way they do. Using open-ended questions keeps the conversation going and helps you move through different topics to learn more about the other person. You build rapport by matching facial expressions and body language to the other person and mentioning their name multiple times throughout a conversation.

3. Have a sense of humor. Being fun and likable is also a big part of nurturing connectivity. However, humor needs to be authentic to your personality and suitable to the occasion. One of the great ways to develop a natural, unique sense of humor is to study the style of comedians you like the most and then think about how you can implement their style into your daily conversations.

4. Be considerate and empathetic. Empathy is an amazing ability to put yourself into the shoes of the other person and understand how they think and feel. In the majority of situations, I'd say that people tend to be impressed by those who show care and consideration and turned off by those who are overly self-involved. But how do you make this distinction when your goal is to showcase your personality or skills? This is a great thought-provoker because it could help you solve many internal conflicts around how and why being successful doesn't mean that others have to fail. Connecting with other people by paying attention to their needs doesn't take away the focus from you. Quite the opposite, you become the center of attention because now the other person sees you as someone who understands them. This, too, needs to be genuine because people are good at noticing those who pretend to be helpful only to try and manipulate. The people you meet as you climb up the career ladder will distinguish a genuine attitude from a fake one. There are many great ways to practice empathy because it isn't only a feeling. Empathy is a mental and emotional ability, a muscle you can train the same way you can train your abs.

From empathy, you gain a better understanding of mutual goals, more functional communication, and easier conflict solving. Many other valuable skills arise from simply seeing through people's defense mechanisms. Say you apply for a job, and the interviewer notices that you are considerate and empathetic. What does that tell them? It shows that you can understand work dynamics and other people's direct and hidden intentions. The moment your coworkers realize that, they'll know they can trust you with more demanding work tasks, as you can balance the workflow and prevent toxicity or conflicts from arising in a workgroup.

Now that you know the skills you need to "break the ice," you can make people feel more comfortable and open up more easily, which is essential in becoming a charismatic leader.

Learn How to Remember People's Names

Not everyone is good at remembering names, but there are times in your life when it's necessary. Sometimes forgetting someone's name can even become a problem. For example, introducing yourself and your coworkers to other people can go awkward if, let's say, you can't remember the names of the people you're with. A part of being charismatic (and a quite important one) is to make the people around you feel important. The first way to do it is, for starters, to know their names.

If you have trouble remembering people's names, you should work on it because having someone forget their name can make people around you feel unimportant.

Knowing someone's name, on the other hand, is one of the essential persuasion tools. Addressing a person by their name makes the conversation more personal, and it helps people to open up to hearing your ideas.

Now, let's say that you're someone who has trouble remembering names. If you want to change that, the first thing you need to know is why you have this problem in the first place. Our unconscious minds trigger "danger signals" each time we're in an unfamiliar situation. While people who are just introducing themselves might look completely comfortable and confident, their unconscious minds are anxious and, in fact, afraid (Cohen, 1990).

Nowadays, we love getting to know new people, and it's almost always a good, positive situation in our lives. But for our ancient ancestors, this was a potentially dangerous situation. In 2020, we get to know people because we want to bond with them, while some 20,000 years back in history, a primal human would have an entire ritual of exchanging different signs and behaviors to determine whether the other primate is a friend or a foe (Cohen, 1990). We skip through that whole process and move straight into handshakes, so the names said along the way slip by us. When you forget people's names, it simply means that you experience a momentary "stranger danger" physiological reaction, but there are some things you can do to change this.

Another reason why remembering names can be challenging is that our brains are primarily focused on remembering faces. If you think about it, when you meet another person, you're mainly focused on figuring out or noticing their face and other important information (e.g., age, gender, and their place in the hierarchy of the group).

That being said, the answer to how you can start remembering people's names is a quite simple one: focus on it. When you're introducing yourself to new people, make a conscious effort to listen, remember, and repeat their name. That, of course, can be done in quite natural ways that spark conversations. For example, after another person tells you their name, and let's say you're still shaking hands, introduce a question like, "Hi, [name], how are you doing?" or "Nice to meet you, [name]."

During the first couple of minutes of conversation, try repeating the name once or twice—not too much, though, because it might come across as strange. Another way to remember people's names, of course, when the situation is appropriate is to ask a person to spell their name out or use a mnemonic device. The first is appropriate when the conversation isn't very casual. It's also suitable when you're writing down information, filling out forms, or having some other type of formal interaction where another person is providing their info.

When you have people's names written down, you can use a mnemonic device, which is a technique with which you associate a person's name to another similar or memorable word or phrase. Another way to make remembering people's names easier is to associate them with other familiar people, faces, and objects. Say you meet a woman named Jasmine. What better way to remember it than by visualizing the flower itself?

Simply committing to making an effort to remember people's names usually helps focus on it more. The main reason why you have issues remembering names is that your mind goes somewhere else during introductions. Putting a conscious effort into staying in the present moment helps.

How to Be a Good Listener

Charismatic people are devoted to listening to others, which makes people around them feel understood. Being a good listener is the next most important trait of a charismatic leader. It conveys interest into what another person is talking about, signaling that you value them and the things they're trying to say.

If you don't think of yourself as a prime listener out there, the fault is not entirely on you, and it doesn't mean you're egocentric or self-involved. A lot of the time (and particularly when we're busy or stressed), we're more focused on our own issues and find it more difficult to focus on what the people around us are talking about. Luckily, there are many great ways for you to gain great listening skills:

1. Be present in the moment. Don't let your mind wander off in different directions, but decide to stay focused on the conversation. The effort counts here because staying focused will take some time to learn, particularly if you're stressed and in a hurry. Either way, make sure to maintain eye contact with the person who is talking, and by all means, avoid looking out the window or looking at your phone.

2. Summarize their message. The best way to make a person feel heard is to sum up what they just said, making sure you got everything right. This is also good to avoid miscommunications.

3. Don't interrupt. Wait patiently until another person is finished talking before you start talking. Interrupting is a spontaneous habit, and the more you practice, the more you encourage it. However, the more you stop yourself when you're about to interrupt, the easier it will get over time. If you must interrupt someone to take a call or because you're in a rush, make sure to apologize before saying what you're about to say.

4. Listen with your eyes and face. Eye contact and facial expressions can tell whether or not you're listening, and it shows how you feel and what you think while the other person is talking. While you don't have to maintain constant eye contact, aim to maximize it, and then break it naturally when you're trying to process or visualize what the other person is talking about. When it comes to facial expressions, attune them to the occasion and the emotion of the conversation. A natural way to do this is by empathizing with another person, which is particularly healthy if you have trouble controlling anxious thoughts.

5. Incorporate head movements. Nodding and tilting your head are great ways to show that you're listening. These movements should flow naturally through the conversation. They are a sign that you are processing and understanding what another person is saying.

6. Move your body. You can slightly tilt toward the person, which shows your focus on their story. However, use this movement cautiously as you don't want to intrude on another person's private space. This movement is appropriate when you're sitting. Another important tip is to point your entire body, head to toe, to the person you're talking to. If you're in a group, make sure to turn your body toward the group.

7. Give affirming remarks. Phrases like "I see," "That's great," "I understand," and others are important to remain an active participant in the conversation and not just a passive listener.

8. Ask questions. Asking questions in a conversation shows your interest in the topic and what the other person is trying to say. However, it's crucial that these questions are natural and logical. They should reflect a genuine interest in the answer.

Summary

In this chapter, you learned how to harvest the fruits of careful listening to get people to open up and trust you and, ultimately, remember you. You'll need listening skills to advance in all areas of life, including leadership. You learned that to become an active listener, you need to do the following:

- Develop listening skills by staying present in the moment of conversation. Focus on what the other person is saying and show interest in their words.
- Remember people's names. To truly engage and leave a good impression, you can't afford to forget people's names. Remembering names is made easier by repeating a person's name multiple times during a conversation and using associations and mnemonic tools to recall the names that are hard to retain in your memory.
- Be a good listener. Listening isn't just absorbing other people's words; it is also about making them feel like they're being

heard. For this, you have to listen more than speak. Mimic another person's body language. Move your head to show that you're paying attention. Summarize their words. Ask questions and give answers.

Chapter 4: How to Small Talk

In leadership, small talk is an integral part of networking. It helps you make positive first impressions and become an influential leader. More importantly, it requires and boosts social skills. Introverts may not enjoy this part of networking, but it helps build rapport and connect with new customers, peers, and coworkers to climb to the top. When discussing making small talk in leadership, it's important to remember that how you feel on the inside shines through your appearance. The very anticipation of awkwardness can very well create tension and anxiety, so learning how to overcome it is crucial for good networking.

When thinking about exceptional small talk, it's important not to bother yourself with what you'll say or do, anticipating to say something unintelligent or embarrassing yourself. While you should have your conversations planned out, you shouldn't entirely focus on this part of the process. Aside from this, be authentic and avoid asking common lazy questions people hear about most of the time they meet someone new. At least you shouldn't start a conversation like that. Instead, start with something unique and original, perhaps by complimenting a person's outfit or saying something funny about the venue. For example, you can ask a person more profound questions about their career choice (e.g., why they chose to work the job they do and what about it that excites them the most).

How to Improve Your Small-Talk Skills

Meeting new people, networking, or spreading your influence hardly ever goes without some small talk. When you don't know new people well, the only suitable topics to talk about are those you have in common, which aren't many in this situation. Not everyone likes small talk, but it's necessary to develop deeper bonds and connections. You may think of small talks as trivial conversations, but they're anything but that. They are necessary to discover common interests with other people, and they lead to more meaningful conversations that people enjoy the most. But how do you become successful with small talk?

1. Be comfortable with yourself first. If you spend minutes or even hours leading up to the event, obsessing over having to chat and meet new people, this will shift your focus from the real purpose of the occasion. Instead, think about why you're going to the event in the first place. Think about the goals and how you want to present yourself. If it's a happy, more relaxed occasion (e.g., a wedding), think about those people whose friendship you're honoring by going to the event and how all people you'll meet there are important to them.

2. Think about people you know who will attend the same event. Meeting new people is a lot easier when there's someone you know to keep you company. Think about the people you have something in common with, and plan to approach them when you arrive at the event.

3. Make it fun. One of the best ways to do small talk is to make a challenge out of it. Set your mind to meet a certain number of new people and spend a specific amount of time chatting. This way, you will be competing with yourself. Moreover, you think less about the anxiety and perhaps awkwardness that go into having these conversations.

4. Show initiative. If you wait for people to approach you, there are good chances that you might meet only a person or two or even no one. On the other hand, if you set your mind to approach people first (and even better, make a task or a challenge out of it), you will become more comfortable being introduced to new acquaintances. Here, it's important not to spend the entire event following the one person you know. Depending on your relationship (and particularly if you're not very close), it can become awkward, and the other person might feel stifled. Instead, branch out and meet other people independently.

5. Remember your task. Whichever event you're going to, you have a certain role. Think about your role and how to do it the best way you can. When you're aware of why you're there, this will give you a point of focus. Now that you know what you aim to do, think about the people who are the best likely companions, and show interest in these people. Aside from that, be approachable, pleasant, and positive. Be your authentic self. Remember, people are very good at detecting authenticity and won't like a person who appears to have a good time but, in fact, looks uninterested when they talk to them.

How to Lead Conversations to Connect and Spread Your Influence

Essentially, small talks are informal conversations that need a little bit of strategizing for those who are shy or don't like meeting new people. Here are a couple of suggestions for making small talk that can build rapport and network:

1. Be a subtle interrogator. Asking questions has been mentioned multiple times in this book. However, it's important to specify what kind of questions you'll ask during small talk. You see, it's imperative to distinguish appropriate questions for formal conversations and those in casual chit-chat. The former requires more profound questions that show your understanding and empathy, and the latter demands a more light-hearted, gentler approach. While chatting, you should ask questions that showcase a spark of interest. However, don't make anyone feel awkward or intrude on their privacy. Your questions should be more general and open-ended, allowing the person to answer in a way that says more about their lifestyle and personality. Next, your questions should be fun, relatable, and suitable to the occasion. It's essential to find something both of you enjoy talking about.

2. Take in the information. Aside from using the active-listening skills mentioned earlier, a casual chat is an excellent opportunity to notice things about people they're less likely to speak directly about. When you listen carefully (particularly during a chat), you can observe not only what the other person likes but also what frustrates them and what they dislike. Moreover, you can conclude about their personality based on that.

3. Show you're interested. Of course, showing you're interested by being actively engaged in the conversation and putting away any distractions and electronics is important to keep the person's attention and interest. Showing enthusiasm to get to know the other person is vital for them to feel comfortable. Most of the time, people worry about imposing themselves on other people, which is why they feel less comfortable chatting and are most likely to end it quickly. When you show genuine interest and make the other person feel important and valued, there's a greater chance that they will remember you.

How to Keep Conversations Going to Avoid Awkward Pauses

Despite having excellent conversation skills, many find it hard to discover appropriate topics for casual chat. At the same time, most people dread the moments of awkward pause when they don't know what to say. Here are some suggestions for potentially great small-talk topics:

1. The environment: You can discuss and comment on the scenery while making sure not to say something disrespectful. Saying positive things about the venue or location helps point out that you're somewhere pleasant and comfortable, which is an emotion the other person will detect.

2. Hobbies and entertainment: You can spark a discussion on what both of you enjoy doing in your free time—for example, watching movies, reading, exercising, or training a sport. Try your best to keep the talk away from discussing work, particularly if it's not relevant to the situation. Some people find talking about work stressful and may withdraw from the conversation because of it.

3. Pleasure: Whatever makes both of you feel amused is a great conversation starter. Food and art are also great options. Everyone eats, which means you can discuss the food being served at the event and move on to talk about favorite foods overall. You can also discuss restaurants and other places you like to visit. If the person you're talking to appreciates art, you can talk about shows, colors, mediums, your favorite artists, and so on.

How to Improve Conversation Skills for Memorable Conversations

As you can see, there are many topics to chat about that can be pleasant and fun for you and the other person. If you're still not convinced in the value of small talk, here are some more strategies to improve your social skills:

1. Talk with purpose. All conversations have a purpose, and so does small talk. While the topics you're discussing may not be important or very interesting, they serve to take the pressure off certain situations. Particularly, it reduces the pressure to sound smart.

2. Aim to make people feel comfortable. Pay attention to whether the things you say make people feel more comfortable and at ease, or they introduce tension. When you focus on saying things that are encouraging and display compassion, you can help a person feel comfortable around you even when the situation itself isn't comfortable.

3. Stay in the moment. One of the most difficult obstacles to overcome is to stop thinking about the things that bother you and just immerse yourself in the present moment. If you have trouble staying away from anxious thoughts, remember the fact that thinking about these things won't solve your problems. When an anxious thought appears, remember that there's nothing you can do about it at that moment. Hence, there's no reason why you should allow it to ruin an opportunity to make new acquaintances. Also, avoid focusing too much on your posture, tone, and the way you speak. This will make you even more self-conscious and break the subtle yet pleasant course of the conversation.

4. *Aim to understand what the other person is interested in.* This will prevent awkward silence and make it easier to find out what to say and which topic to bring up. To do this, ask not only open-ended but also more engaging questions that spark more complex answers—for example, what the other person likes about their career or what their hobbies or interests are. If the other person says something you find interesting, ask them about it, and inquire about specific details you find intriguing or amusing.

5. Follow up with more engaging questions. Don't let the conversation die after the other person finished talking. Instead, you can keep the course of the conversation going by stating your commentary, mentioning something similar that happened to you or that is relatable in some other way. Then follow up with another logical or interesting question. Participating in the conversation with your own observations and experiences will prevent the other person from feeling like they're being interrogated.

6. Share relevant information about yourself too. Of

course, you don't have to share too much, but things like your name, occupation, a general location, and other information are important so that the other person has more details to remember you by. Many people are uncomfortable sharing personal details like their address or where their children go to school, and that's fine. While you should aim to reciprocate the amount of information the other person gave out, it doesn't have to be the same type of information. For example, if your acquaintance said where they go for a medical checkup, and you don't want to reveal this information, you can say where you go for a haircut or mention other details later in the conversation. Still, make sure that the course of the conversation remains uninterrupted and natural, giving information that seems relevant to the topic. Giving information doesn't only make you more memorable but also more relatable. It helps another person paint a picture of who you are and what you do, and you become more than a name associated with a face in their mind. This creates conditions to bond and keep the conversation going.

Summary

In this chapter, you learned that small talk not only leaves a memorable first impression but also extends your network and achieves personal and business goals. The following are the ways to do this:

- *Enjoying small talk:* You learned that to improve the skills of casual conversations, you first need to be comfortable in your own skin and just have fun. No one will talk to a person who looks like they're being forced to talk to them by a shotgun. If you want people to like you, make them feel like you enjoy being around them.

- *Being a bit sneaky:* Creating a bond with the other person and extending your influence will require sleek observation and evaluation of their character. Detect subtle cues and information about another person's character, motivations, intentions, and knowledge by observing how and what they speak. See whether they are consistent with their appearance and actions. This will tell you a great deal about this person's hidden needs, aspirations, and concerns, which you can later use to your advantage.

- *Being engaged.* Keeping small talk going depends on your skill to find common and interesting topics. Using body language that shows your interest in the conversations, asking smart questions, and juggling different topics (common interests, backgrounds, the setting, and the social occasion) will help maintain the connection between you and other people.

- *Deepening the bond and staying memorable.* The goal of small talk is for the other person to remember you. This is best done by making them feel comfortable, asking open-ended questions, being present, showing interest in what the other person is saying, and of course, sharing memorable and personable information about yourself.

Chapter 5: Storytelling

The main reasons why storytelling in leadership is so important are that stories inspire people to act, they help spread the word about you, your competence and influence, and they help people remember you. One of the reasons why people remember stories so well is that they are based on learning from experience, and our minds are hardwired to learn like that. Your listener's mind will want to remember what you said when you shared your experience, even when they might not be aware of it.

Why You Need to Be a Good Storyteller

Storytelling spreads inspirational ideas, and it helps demonstrate those ideas by using existing motivations and cultural knowledge to solve problems for a person or a group of people. These are the ways storytelling helps leaders:

1. It manages conflicts. Stories give an emotional, experiential background to what you're trying to say.

When people are in conflict, they are emotionally charged and unable to receive direct helpful suggestions. The great thing about storytelling is that it helps convey a message indirectly in a way that is more subtle so that a tense, irritated person may find it easier to accept it. Because of this, sharing a leader's experiences has become an essential step in handling work and personal life issues, as well as addressing problems. At times, saying what you want using different experiences helps people accept what they don't want to hear because they are not the topic, and neither criticism nor instructions are directed toward them.

2. It helps plan the future by learning from the past.
Leadership is all about following dreams, fulfilling visions, and accepting challenges and obstacles along the way. Storytelling can also be used to represent or visualize how a future with one's goals accomplished might look like. If you think about it, the best way to persevere through challenges is to have a truly vivid picture of what you're going after in your mind, and the best way to do this is to simply tell yourself a story. Apart from that, stories involve details (e.g., settings, events, characters, smells, and tastes) that help you feel like you're already experiencing the things you're visualizing. This enables you to keep your vision alive by being able to tap into the entire experience whenever you want to.

3. It influences people through the use of reasoning. As mentioned earlier, storytelling helps people accept things they otherwise wouldn't. This is because stories offer more meaning and depth. They create room to convey rational, reasonable messages that people may not like hearing but, in a way, creates an emotional response. When you try to pass your message using plain facts and numbers, there's a chance that the listeners won't relate much with what you're saying. However, when you wrap this information into a story, it becomes emotional, personal, interesting, and meaningful. As a result, people remember the information they heard.

How to Tell a Convincing Story

Aside from knowing the right way to tell a story, it's also important to include the crucial elements that make the story convincing. The main aspects of telling a story that convinces people in your message will include context, metaphors/analogies, feelings, physical elements, and a surprise twist. These elements should be wrapped into a story told in a style that is suitable for business settings. These types of stories are usually told in a speedy, punchy way, with a positive twist or a funny remark in the end, if possible. Your story shouldn't last longer than five minutes, or else you might lose your listener's attention.

But how do you know which story to share with your audience? First, think about the key messages, projects, or experiences you want to share that are relevant to your audience. Which of your past experiences and projects are related to the particular situation? Your examples can include both successes and failures, as long as the lesson is relevant, useful, and beneficial to the audience. Other elements of the story can be used to enhance your point. Don't be afraid of investing time and effort into planning what you will say and how you will say it.

Being a great storyteller undoubtedly expands your influence and helps people bond with you. It makes you more relatable and personable. Knowing how to tell and share stories can make you an attention magnet and become a tool you can use to meet new people and spread your message more effectively. It can help you connect with a group and establish yourself as a leader. Here are a couple of elements of storytelling to keep in mind:

The story arc: This is the first element of storytelling to master. It includes saying the details that build up the story and create interest and intrigue, adding a twist to make a story memorable. When you're building up a story, focus on starting with casual details so that the tension, or the point of conflict, sounds more interesting. Include details of how you felt being in a particular setting or a situation that led up to the event in question. Describe how you felt, what you did, and what the other characters of the plot did. These details help you paint a picture of what you're talking about, making it more vivid in the minds of those who listen.

The hook: There has to be an element that will spark the listener's interest to stay engaged throughout the story. Whether it's a funny story or a tense one, adding the hook will build up people's attention before you add a plot twist. To make the story more memorable, act a bit out of character, and emphasize certain peculiarities about people's mannerisms and personality. Of course, make sure you're not disrespectful or offensive. Depending on the situation, you can decide whether or not to imitate accents, body language, and other little kinks that could add to the appeal of the story. However, make sure not to overuse these elements, or else you could come across as being fake or over the top. Unless you're making a career doing stand-up comedy, keep in mind that you still want to stay authentic and relatable.

The punchline: This will be the highlight of the story, and it will summarize its entire message and vibe into one or two sentences. One of my favorite comedians, Kevin Hart, once told a story that perhaps wouldn't be at all funny hadn't he imitated the posture of an ostrich. Essentially, Kevin told a simple story of how his friend threw a can at the bird, and it got angry. But he kept repeating how the bird's body pointed forwards and his head sideways. As he narrated how the ostrich came after him and his friend, Kevin's punchline (with an imitation) was "Its body was like this [standing straight and turning its side to the audience], but its head was like THIS [turns his head toward the audience with an angry, blank expression on this face]." To this day, I can't rationally explain what's particularly funny about this joke, but I keep rewatching Kevin time after time because I just want to get to that part of the story.

What can we learn from this example? Kevin used this

punchline to paint a picture of the entire ridiculousness of the situation and show how it unveiled differently from what was expected. The punchline set the stage for the twist, which was you can't run away from an angry ostrich, not even in a car. The bird kept chasing the two men while they were driving away, and the joke ended on an ambiguous note. Did it ever catch them? The twist to the story is the element of surprise that completely changes the direction of the story.

As you can see, there's nothing particularly hard or complicated about good storytelling. Still, you might need some exercise if you're not particularly keen on being the center of attention. Attune your humor or drama style to that of the audience.

Being a good storyteller is essential because all leaders build their charisma around their experiences, whether it's success or failure. Those who look up to you do so because of what you represent and how your experiences relate to theirs; it's not necessarily about who you are. The best way to connect and engage with those around you is to tell stories that spark interest, motivate, and inspire.

How to Make Your Story Memorable

In leadership, stories have a role of enlightening the mood, reliving a situation, appealing to potential followers, and gaining their approval. In a nutshell, if you want to win people over, your story needs to become their story.

The first criterion for this is that the story is interesting. The topic and the events need to be relevant to your group and appropriate for the occasion. Here, you need to use smart, well-thought-through exaggerations in strategically chosen places to win over the audience. Too few, and your story won't be memorable. Too many, and your listeners will miss the main point.

As someone striving to become a charismatic leader, you should have multiple stories prepared beforehand for the situations in which you'll be asked to tell a story. Think about the potentially inspiring events from your life and career. Figure out the ways to tell them things that are positive, charming, and entertaining but still realistic and authentic. Leave out those parts that seem irrelevant or have proven to be irrelevant for the main point of the story.

To showcase charisma, you'll need to develop a talent for making an average story great. People tend to get excited about stories that mix sad with humorous events, as those feel more realistic and personable. The main point of your story should be clearly stated at the end of it, although it's a good idea to make the audience look back and try to establish the connection between the events they were told about. As you take your listeners through the most important lessons from your story, keep them engaged using humor and detailed verbal description of how you felt in a situation and what made you feel like that.

Another important thing to focus on is to know how to use your voice in terms of narration, tone, pauses, pace, and emphasis on words that reflect the most relevant aspects of the story. Being prepared, looking put together, and memorizing your story in advance will help you engage more with your listeners because you won't have to stop to remember what you wanted to say. Also, you won't disengage because you're talking while remembering what to say next at the same time.

Body language is another important element of storytelling. Your head, eyes, posture, hands, and legs need to move along with the story and reflect its emotion and course. You should add an element of drama to your performance but still in a leveled, authentic way. If your goal is for your listeners to remember your story as a realistic, relatable one and not observe it similarly to an acting performance, you should use these elements strategically to emphasize important aspects of the story. Body language, in this case, only serves to reinforce the story and not necessarily become the main focus.

In terms of learning how to grow your charisma, storytelling serves to help you break out of your comfort zone. It helps you grow and develop confidence and convert your own feelings to another person. If you feel nervous about being in front of other people, it is very likely that other people will also pick up on your feelings. They will feel nervous around you and may even avoid being around you. However, if you feel good and confident, you will radiate this feeling, and people will pick up on that as well.

How to Tell Personal Stories

People will want to be around you if you make them feel good, and that's the truth. By learning how to be a good storyteller, you will learn how to influence people's emotions as well. However, you will only achieve this if your story appears believable and authentic. It should spark genuine interest. But how do you do this?

First, look back at your *experiences*. Think about the most important and most memorable success, failure, happy, and sad stories you can remember. Your stories will have to have a correct, truthful, genuine base that you will later embellish to prove a point and trigger different feelings.

Once you find stories you want to showcase, polish them to *make them more memorable*. Here, you will work on recalling the details about the settings and people who participate in the events. Add context, like telling more about your background and how that affected the events. These elements will add impact to the story and make it more memorable.

After you've done that, think about the *structure* of your story for a while. Each story has three main parts, which include the context (the beginning), the conflict (the middle), and the resolution (the end). The beginning will serve to present the listener with the context, background, settings, and character. In the middle part of your story, you will introduce obstacles and twists. Then you move to the resolution. You will resolve the story in the end, where you'll explain how the characters got or didn't get what they want.

When thinking about telling great stories, you should *focus on obstacles* that came in the way of either you or other characters achieving their goal. This will help engage the listeners emotionally. Each obstacle should have a potential solution, and it is up to you to decide whether or not it is a successful one. Most appealing stories have obstacles whose surpassing usually leads to further twists. Sometimes these obstacles have both positive and negative results.

Finally, it's time to focus on how you tell your story. When you're telling a story in person, it should be shorter because the listeners are likely to lose their interest after a while. Only tell the essential parts of the story using carefully chosen elements of embellishment and drama to truly highlight the most important elements. For this, it's important to use expressions of emotion and pauses thoughtfully. This emphasizes the message and maximizes emotional engagement. How you'll use these elements depends on the story itself.

Summary

In this chapter, you learned how to be a captivating storyteller to influence people around you and get your message across. You learned the following:

- You need to be a good storyteller if you want people to be influenced by your message. You learned that storytelling is a must in leadership, and it helps people associate memories and feelings with your message. It also helps them remember you and connect on a deeper level.

- You need to tell a convincing story if you want people to believe what you're saying. You learned that to be compelling, a story must be based on the truth but also embellished to make it more appealing and memorable. You learned that each story has an arc, a hook, a twist, and a punchline. These elements give structure to your story and help keep the listeners engaged.

- You make stories memorable using tone of voice, body language, and examples that are suitable and relevant to the situation.

Telling personal stories helps not only spread your message but also establish yourself as a trustworthy, friendly person that people will want to connect with.

Chapter 6: Presence and Magnetism

In one of the previous chapters, we talked about growing personal charisma. Now, we'll talk about taking your appeal to the next level. Magnetism is a quality that not only makes people like you but also draws them to you. It drives people to follow you, as they want to be a part of your communities and listen to what you have to say. But how do you become magnetically appealing to other people?

Magnetism is a quality that people with the ability to steal the spotlight possess. It is an attractive quality that can be used both for good and bad purposes. In this book, I'll share advice on nurturing genuine, authentic personal attractiveness that stems from a healthy mentality and not narcissistic or sociopathic tendencies to abuse others for one's own purposes. More precisely, I'll talk about developing the type of charisma that grows from a desire to love and serve your idea of the greatest good.

Some people are born with this quality, while others need to learn. Either way, in this chapter, you will learn how to develop a magnetic aura that draws people in. The first quality required for this is personal charisma. Charisma is often hard to describe, and it stems both from personal traits and from exterior looks and assets. Some people are attractive because of their looks; others for their intellect. However, there are also those whose personality is appealing.

In previous chapters, we discussed the methods and techniques for developing personal charisma and becoming more relatable. Now, we will delve deeper into this particular quality. Charisma stems from having a deep, healthy relationship with yourself. You will only be charismatic if you are truly confident and convinced in your own value and competence. Charismatic people are usually firm believers. Their faith and values shape their career and personality. Your faith and vision will reach and inspire those around you. But to do this, you first need to work on your belief system and your confidence.

Strategies for Growing Magnetic Charisma

Another essential part of being charismatic is to be charming. Now, *charm* is a trait that takes a bit more work. You must delve deeper into your character and discover how your inner potential to love and contribute to other people's growth can shine through your appearance and behaviors. This way (and particularly if your motivations come from an intention to do good), you will gain followers on your journey. People around you will want to work with you to help fulfill your cause because they see it as their own. Your charm can serve as a powerful tool for motivation and creativity. To do this, you can use a couple of different strategies:

1. Be polished and put together. Charismatic leaders always look and behave their best. Since they have a highly developed self-awareness, they are able to manage their feelings and thoughts in a way that allows them to control what they'll focus on and what they'll think about. As they're in touch with their inner selves, true charismatic leaders are never arrogant or egocentric. Instead, they have a purpose in mind, and they only display those parts of themselves that agree with their purpose. Of course, no one is flawless, and we're all people. However, those who strive toward being leaders carefully choose when and how to open up and speak about their issues. In other words, they confide in their friends behind closed doors.

2. Focus on others. Leaders are often in the spotlight, but their focus is on other people. This way, the energy between them and their followers becomes reciprocal. For this reason, their followers stick around. If you think about it, when leaders focus on solving others' problems, they give their energy to them. In return, their followers reciprocate but put in the work that serves the leader's purpose. Of course, it is always possible for this pattern to become manipulative or even criminal. Genuine leaders are led by the motivation to change this world and the people around them for the better.

3. *Develop your conversation skills.* People who possess a magnetic appeal have excellent *conversation* skills. They balance listening and speaking carefully. First, they listen to what others have to say and then respond with well-thought-out stories that share their wisdom, experience, and useful knowledge. Everything they say has a purpose, even if they talk about their passion, hobbies, and interests. Charismatic leaders are skillful storytellers who use their language skills and mannerisms to convey powerful messages. For this, they engage only in profound, meaningful, and important topics, avoiding offensive and controversial issues.

4. *Pay attention to nonverbal language.* Charismatic leaders pay attention to others' nonverbal language. What we detect from body language has a subliminal impact on the interaction. It affects how we feel and what we deduce from the conversation. Assertive body language, good eye contact, and carefully strategized physical contact are all tools that charismatic leaders use to connect with their followers.

5. *Develop empathy.* *Empathy* is an essential power behind authentic charisma. People are drawn to those who love and feel for them on instinct. However, where this connection will go (whether or not it will be healthy, productive, and growth-supportive) depends on how you wield it. Being empathetic means knowing how to put yourself in others' shoes and knowing what's healthy, appropriate, and helpful.

How to Influence People with Your Magnetic Presence

Charisma is a trait that can get you far in life. It can help you land jobs, conquer the love of your life, and find your way out of a speeding ticket. Some people say it even gets them free pizza every once in a while. However, rarely anyone is simply born with this trait. People who are raised to have strong confidence and self-respect may show it even as toddlers. In contrast, others become charismatic later in life once they realize where their true passions and devotions lie and become aware of their infinite value.

Scientists are yet to unveil the mystery behind charisma. What we know is that it is a learned behavior. It's not a gene that you are gifted with that makes you famous and loved. The so-called charisma is learned early in life and has a significant impact on one's success in adulthood.

No matter how objective and unbiased the modern world strives to be, charismatic people somehow manage to appeal to those who are in deciding positions, earning business opportunities and promotions that don't always stem strictly from their skillset or credentials. This is because charismatic people know how to influence people. Oftentimes, this knowledge is instinctive, and these people are good at noticing how to behave and what to say to ease other people into giving them what they want. This quality is highly effective in industries related to sales, art, and creativity, wherein appealing to people's unspoken needs and feelings plays a deciding role in making a profit.

Those who've studied charisma as a trait have determined that there are three common traits that help charismatic people influence others:

- *Being down-to-earth*: People with appealing personalities are attractive due to their "present" nature. Unlike those whose mindset revolves around past regrets and future plans, charismatic people live in the here and now. They address current issues with boldness and confidence.
- *Kindness*: Charismatic people have a loving aura around them. Their warmth makes people feel comfortable and open up to their ideas and suggestions.

- *Competence.* Charismatic people usually have a great deal of personal power because they also put in a lot of work into nurturing their talents and abilities and take driven but reasonable action to profit from them.

But what is the one thing that can destroy charisma? The answer is self-doubt. People who have low confidence and insufficient self-esteem avoid eye contact and have a slouched, closed-off posture. They smile less, and when they do, it's usually only on the surface or out of nervousness. All these behaviors combine to say to other people that this person isn't someone they want to connect with. If you think you don't have enough personal charisma, there are things that you can do to change that.

1. Set your mind to be firm and decisive. Decisiveness means to spend less time worrying about things that can possibly go wrong and more time doing everything you can to advance and improve. Taking opportunities whenever you can is also a trait of charismatic people. They don't give up on a job application because they're not sure if they have a chance. They apply for jobs because they want them and think they deserve them. Social intelligence is a secret condiment of their career success, as they use other tools to advance beyond their skill set and level of expertise.

2. Be honest. The second important trait of charismatic people is their *honesty*. They speak their mind, but in a way, that's helpful and respectful. Their honesty is one of the main reasons why people trust them so much.

3. Inspire others without boasting. Charismatic people enjoy sharing the stories of how their *potentials* and drive resulted in astonishing achievements instead of boasting about the accomplishments themselves. For example, a charismatic leader won't talk much about their current post or their salary, but they will talk about the number of hours they put into learning the skills needed to get there or finish a project that was valuable to the company's vision.

4. Encourage people to be in the spotlight. Charismatic people want to hear others' stories and inspire people to talk about themselves. If you think about Oprah, for example, her whole career revolves around helping people improve their lives. She has hosted hundreds of shows focusing on other people's problems and looking for solutions.

How to Speak so That You Command Attention

Influential people also enjoy talking about themselves. This helps other people associate with them and connect easier since they've already shared so much about their own lives.

Confidence is another trait of influential people. People don't find insecurity attractive, but those who appear strong and reliable win their trust quickly and easily. People gravitate toward those they can rely on, even if it's only mentally through a screen. If you learn how to communicate the right way, people will want to connect to your knowledge and expertise. While building confidence isn't a simple thing to do, it's not impossible either. Gaining experience in the areas of expertise and following your passions to express your creativity will build up your sense of competence and help you learn how to trust your abilities. This will take practice and, admittedly, can't be done overnight.

Practicing not only confidence skills but also other personal and career skills will help you learn how to solve your own problems as well as other people's. All of this combined will build up your sense of unique authenticity over time. Confidence also affects how you communicate nonverbally, how you carry yourself, how you maintain eye contact, and how you use your body language. For example, a good measure of eye contact can make or break a connection. Too little or too much is uninviting or can come across as unnatural and strange. But people with true confidence instinctively know when to look and when to look away, which makes their interactions spontaneously successful. They don't have to scan their entire body to convey charismatic mannerisms—they do that intuitively.

Confidence is also essential if you want to be a good listener. Insecure people often overthink how they look and what they're saying, which makes them come across as closed off or inhibited. On the other hand, confident people are truly present in the moment. They listen to what other people say, not only because they aim to influence but also because their entire mindset revolves around genuine interest for people's concerns and the values they stand for. This makes them great listeners and great in engaging in memorable conversations that leave people feeling like they've never had a conversation like that in their life. They are active listeners and go beyond just being quiet and nodding. They process and analyze the things they hear, and they are good at reading between the lines and understanding unspoken messages.

Aside from understanding what's being said directly, charismatic people look into the background of what the other person is saying. They check whether the details of their story are consistent. Are there things that are being left out? What does the omission of these details say about the other person? Is there insecurity or shame they're trying to hide? Is there a way to help them overcome these feelings? More importantly, charismatic people are quite good at recognizing people's needs and desires.

The more you study human interactions, the better you'll understand how people's speech gives away subtle details about their personality. For example, you'll know whether they're confident or whether they care about being loved and accepted. Moreover, details about what their insecurities are, and what they think about people in their lives, can all be picked up just by listening and analyzing what the person is talking about.

However, this requires not only listening but also observing. Much like Sherlock Holmes, charismatic people are good at noticing details about people's clothes, hairstyles, accessories, mannerisms, and other relevant details to find out more about their personality and lifestyle.

Charismatic people are also good at analyzing other people's body language. Body language shows how a person feels (e.g., whether or not they're comfortable, confident, or insecure) and much more.

Charismatic people also possess emotional warmth. They smile (but this isn't a form of a well-rehearsed smile), have an inviting glance in their eyes, and tilt in slightly as they talk. These are all results of their unconscious minds. Charismatic people tap into that inner sense of happiness and comfort they want to spread to the world around them, which also reflects in their body posture and facial expressions.

Now that you know what it means to be charismatic and how to get there, you probably understand that this is something you can't fake. True charisma comes from a strong connection with your inner self and, more importantly, a sense of unconditional personal value. It enables you to notice other people's infinite value, and it creates an atmosphere of trust.

When people feel like they can trust you, they will also form a lasting bond with you. This is greatly affected by your state of mind. How you feel about yourself is the ultimate mystery to solve, and embarking on that journey starts when you look into your deepest beliefs, fears, and desires. It takes looking into your own goals and expectations to truly begin appreciating yourself so that others find you approachable and personable as well.

Summary

In this chapter, you learned how to start nurturing authentic charisma to appeal to people and spread your influence using the following strategies:

- Being put together, polished, attentive, empathetic, and skillful in conversations
- Listening to people and paying attention to their mannerisms, hidden needs, and motives
- Spreading your messages in a genuine, measured, accurate, and authentic way

Chapter 7: Being Assertive

Do you feel like you're constantly sacrificing your time and effort to accommodate other people? Do you feel like you're saying yes when you want to say no just to avoid confrontation? If so, you're not alone. Most people are raised to think (even if only unconsciously) that saying no is something bad, and putting your needs and goals ahead of other people is selfish. While that couldn't be further from the truth, many of us overly accommodate other people.

Develop Social Assertiveness and Get What You Need and Want Out of Interactions

Whether it's business or relationships, many people think that having your own boundaries and preserving your integrity is selfish and wrong. If you want to become successful and influential, you're going to have to learn how to overcome this notion.

But how will you stop accommodating other people and sacrificing your time and effort to do other people's work or fix other people's errors if you feel like you're being selfish or irresponsible if you don't do so? The answer is by learning about becoming more assertive.

Perhaps you are unable to say no to your boss or return a cold meal at the restaurant. You must know that the inability to stand up for yourself can cost you and everyone else around you. If not in time and money, the cost is being unable to do your best work and focus your energy on the activities that lead to growth because you are doing mundane chores that are truly irrelevant in the long run.

Assertiveness Isn't a Personality—It's a Skill

The inability to establish healthy boundaries results from being afraid of disappointing other people and being rejected. And perhaps, people who don't stand up to their superiors at work fear the possibility of losing their jobs. Sometimes people will even sacrifice their hobbies and interests just so as not to let down certain people. These fears all come from quite innate fears of rejection. Once you realize that your fears have nothing to do with the prospect of real-life consequences, you'll start to look at these situations from a different perspective. Having a respectful but firm heart-to-heart with those who push your boundaries doesn't have to be inappropriate or awkward. It can be done in ways that allow the other person to understand how their behavior affects you, and more importantly, it conveys that your message and decision are final.

Being unable to say no sometimes means that you have the "nice guy/girl" syndrome. This syndrome includes numerous traits, behaviors, and attitude characteristics of people who take a passive approach to life, giving everyone around them the power to make their decisions and occupy their time and schedule. Oftentimes, you find it hard to say no even when the demands are unreasonable or harmful for you, simply out of fear that you will anger or affect others. As you may notice, this is most certainly not a healthy nor helpful trait. By being a nice guy/girl, you're not really helping anyone.

If you think about it, your behaviors don't allow people to see the true consequences of their actions. Beneath all this lies the problem with anxiousness and low self-esteem, which leads to building up resentment for people around you, even the closest ones.

Have you ever accommodated friends and family members only to realize you cringe as soon as they call and that you avoid picking up the phone because you can't stand having another conversation with them? This feeling doesn't always result from the traits of that particular person or their true toxicity. Often, your inability to speak your mind makes you feel as if the person has expectations they actually don't have. You're thinking about those individuals as intrusive and unpleasant to be around. The longer this lasts, the greater the chances of your relationship ending in flames.

The worst consequence of being unable to stand up for yourself is the reluctance to focus on your dreams and goals. Because you think (at least unconsciously) that other people will be offended and feel abandoned if you choose to focus on yourself, you sacrifice your dreams. As you can assume, this has little chance of ending well. It can make you feel stuck and helpless. As suppressed needs, feelings, and thoughts build, you eventually start to carry resentment. The more you feel like other people are taking advantage of you, the more you're likely to burst into a rage or even violence. Now, that's not a good way to go through life, isn't it?

To stop thinking and acting in this way, you'll have to learn to become more proactive and assume more control over your life. Rather than shifting from one extreme to another, you can start learning how to stay in the middle of the spectrum between complete passiveness and destructive aggressiveness. This position is also called assertiveness.

How to Start Training to Be Assertive

Assertiveness is more than simple confidence training. Typically, men are taught to be more in touch with their emotions, while women are taught to be more confident. However, this is an oversimplification of what it means to be assertive. Assertiveness is a complex interpersonal skill of nurturing healthy confidence in ways that are respectful to both yourself and other people's boundaries. Being assertive means being honest. It means speaking your mind about things that bother you, as well as those you want or don't want. This is because you will stop assuming what people think. The more you realize how off your assumptions can be, the more you understand the importance of being truthful.

However, assertiveness skills also help you convey your opinion in ways that help find common ground. They don't leave much space for misinterpretation. For example, you'll learn how to speak your mind in ways that won't necessarily upset a person or hurt their feelings. You will learn how to communicate in ways that help reach a compromise. This way, you will understand how to go after what you want without fear that it will make you lonely or hurt those around you.

The benefits of being assertive are numerous. Being more assertive improves your relationships and makes them healthier. This will happen because you'll know how to communicate your needs in ways the other person will understand. This will prevent resentment from building up. Aside from that, you will feel less stressed. People who go through assertiveness training develop better strategies to cope with stress. As you learn to turn down requests that put pressure on you and focus more on doing the things you want, you will become less anxious. You will care less about what other people think about you and your opinions, actions, choices, and tastes.

Once you start learning how to become more assertive, you will start feeling like you're more in control of your life. This will help you start building confidence. As you know by now, it's very hard to develop strong confidence when your focus is on the things other people want and not those that you want. Don't allow other people to dictate your actions and occupy your schedule.

When you start paying more attention to what you think and what you want, your decisions and motivations come from a different place, and it's certainly not a selfish one. If you recall, I mentioned that charismatic people have a keen awareness of what they stand for. More often than not, their motives revolve around helping others while doing things that feel good for them too.

Oprah Winfrey has helped dozens. She runs numerous charities and changes others' lives every day. But she gets a spot on the air, luxuries of a convenient life, and social status. Kevin Hart makes people laugh but charges a good amount of money for it. Once you bridge the gap between wanting to contribute and wanting to make yourself happy, your confidence will start to thrive. But to do this, you first need to be aware of personal goals and be in full control of your life goals, which can be done once you become more assertive.

Being more assertive will also help you relieve anger and resentment. These feelings stem from your decisions to accommodate other people, and not necessarily from other people's malice and expectations. Once you become more aware of this (particularly when you devote to doing more of the things you want), you will become more tolerant and feel overall more peaceful and positive. As you can see, the benefits of becoming more assertive are numerous. But how do you get there?

Step 1: Adopt an assertive mindset. The first step toward nurturing assertiveness is to start adopting an assertive mindset. Your task will be to review your beliefs and let go of all inner limitations. The more you do this, the more you'll start to understand how your growth and happiness help everyone else. The more you observe how actions done in the name of selflessness are less helpful than those done for the purpose of personal growth, the more you'll grow a faith that setting healthy boundaries benefits everyone around you. It helps your business, your friends, your family, and your relatives.

Step 2: Start setting healthy boundaries. The next step in becoming more assertive is to learn how to start setting healthy boundaries. Healthy boundaries are a set of limits and rules that define what you're willing or unwilling to allow other people to do. The fewer boundaries you have, the greater the chance of allowing yourself to become a pushover. When you nurture your boundaries, your mindset will shift, and your confidence will grow. This will benefit your health, relationships, and career.

Step 3: Take personal responsibility. Personal responsibility is the other side of the assertive coin. You have *rights* on one side, and *responsibilities* on the other side. Here, I'm not just talking about daily tasks and chores. Responsibility (or better yet, *self-responsibility*) is the trait that helps you look at yourself as in charge of your well-being. People who lack self-responsibility view other people as both a cause and a solution to their problem. This is because they have a passive approach to life. For example, you might be unhappy in a relationship and think the problem is that the other person doesn't pay enough attention to you. But the real problem is that you rely on other people for attention and validation, and the truth could be that you expect more attention from people than they feel comfortable giving. As you learn to become more assertive, you will assume responsibility for your happiness and do more of the things that make you happy on your own. This way, you'll no longer expect other people to make you happy.

Taking responsibility for your problems and actions, as well as their consequences, helps you become more proactive and take action on those things that appear to need changing. Most of the time, people avoid doing the things that solve their problems out of sheer fear of failure. The stronger your confidence, the fewer your excuses will be for not doing or achieving what you want. Assuming responsibility for your problems will help you see how some of your actions contributed to the worsening of your situation, even if a particular issue may not be entirely your fault.

Learning assertiveness will reduce the expectations you have from yourself and everyone else. You will discover that people can't guess what you want and that you, instead, need to communicate your thoughts, needs, and desires if you're going to give people a chance to understand you. Also, you'll begin to see how acting on assumptions can cause a lot of resentment and hurt to both you and everyone else around you. You will also learn how to speak about what you want and how to voice your boundaries in a healthy way.

Aside from this, assertiveness will help you understand that you can't control how other people will think, how they will feel, and what they will do. This can dramatically change how you see relationships. This will help you stop submitting to other people's will and trying to make everyone happy. Perhaps, one of the most important things to learn will be that you are not in charge of making other people happy. You shouldn't set this expectation upon yourself, and other people don't have the right to do that either.

On the other hand, you will also learn how to voice your needs and concerns in ways that don't step on other people's boundaries, sense of integrity, feelings, and dignity. You will learn how to maintain a gentle balance between standing up for yourself and what you believe in and being respectful. You will have to make peace with the fact that people will be unhappy about some of your choices and decisions, but you'll also be able to live with it. However, as you're responsible for the consequences of your words and actions, you'll learn to observe, evaluate, plan for, and consider possible consequences when deciding whether or not to speak your mind.

Techniques and Exercises for Assertiveness

Now that you know why it's essential to learn how to become more assertive, let's dig into some specific exercises you can do each day to nurture an assertive mindset. While some people have a natural talent for assertive behavior and naturally instill trust and autonomy into the ways they talk to other people, others need more help in learning how to communicate to get along with people while maintaining and honoring their identity and integrity. The exercises given in the following sections will help you achieve your goals using inner strength.

First things first, you need to understand that your upbringing may be one of the reasons why you may struggle with an assertive attitude. If you were raised in a way that signaled that expressing your needs is somehow undesirable and burdening, it makes sense that you will proceed with these behaviors in your adult life. Being unassertive means feeling and acting under the influence of confusion surrounding your identity. It means acting on self-doubt, a sense of inferiority, guilt, and shame. Everyone has a passive side and an aggressive side, but learning how to balance those in healthy ways ensures a balanced attitude that will get you where you want to be in life.

Exercise #1: Self-evaluation.

Practicing an assertive attitude starts by *re-evaluating your expectations.* Whether you're too passive or aggressive, you probably have a negative expectation of what's to come. As a result, you act on this negative assumption even when it's inaccurate. At the beginning of your assertive exercises, it's not your behavior you're aiming to change but your thought process. First, imagine a potentially stressful situation. Think about what makes you dread feeling embarrassed or defeated. What is the outcome you're expecting? Now, review how expecting this outcome makes you feel. Are you upset? Do you jump to conclusions, or do you withdraw? What are the things you'll say and do in this situation? Last and most important, what are the responses, both inner and exterior, that you want to change? Do you want to handle a similar situation differently, and how?

Exercise #2: Emotional awareness.

The next step is to *become aware of your feelings and desires.* To become more assertive, start focusing on being aware of what you truly need and want. If this is repressed, you'll feel tense whenever you have a chance of doing something important for you. Additionally, the image of what you think you want might be exaggerated, creating an additionally unachievable goal. To do this, study all human needs (e.g., feeling safe and fed, loved, accepted, meaningful, and fulfilled). Next, create a vision board of how you see those needs manifested in real life. How should your life be so that these needs are fulfilled? Are there things in your life that you might be accepting or denying to protect yourself from negative feelings? Think about how the things you fear relate to those needs that aren't being fulfilled.

Exercise #3: Identify your strengths.

Everyone has some areas of their life where they're more successful in being aware of their needs and are able to identify emotions clearly. Think about your strengths and map out these areas. Recall how you think and feel in situations where you feel strong and capable of overcoming insecurities. How can you transfer these positive behavioral patterns into the other areas of your life? How can you take some of the useful thoughts, feelings, and actions from those areas of your life where you're successful to those where you feel challenged? Based on this, create an action plan on how you'll face challenging situations using the resources you used in cases where you acted assertively, and commit to putting your plan into action. The more you challenge yourself and practice these situations, the more you'll feel confident and competent to handle them.

Exercise #4: Process negative feelings.

The fourth step is to learn how to *work through guilt and shame.* While there are some situations you'll handle with more success; others will result in unfavorable outcomes. Perhaps your crush will reject your invitation on a date. Maybe people don't like seeing you setting boundaries. These are all everyday situations that happen to most people. They don't only happen to you. So ask yourself, how will you process the episodes of feeling embarrassed or beat down after facing an emotional trigger? First, become aware that feelings of anger or resentment often serve to shelter from shame, and it is the shame you're aiming to process. The best way to do that is to rationalize why and how the particular experience is nothing to be ashamed about. Mistakes and failures happen to anyone, and there's no reason for you to feel particularly guilty over any experience.

Exercise #5: Grow personal strength.

The final step in learning how to become more assertive is to grow personal strength. How is this done? The simple answer is by obtaining the resources of strength. What does this mean? It means to exercise appropriate body language, grow your social skills in areas that feel challenging, and learn how to process unpleasant experiences. The main reason behind conflicts in all areas of life is people acting defensively to shelter themselves from feeling guilty and ashamed. It causes aggressiveness, emotional suppression, avoidance, and many other unhealthy behaviors. Instead, practice using more mature, balanced ways to cope with challenges (e.g., using your own resources of gratitude, forgiveness, acceptance, bravery, anticipation, self-regulation, and self-sufficiency).

Summary

In this chapter, you learned just how vital assertiveness is in leadership. You learned that being assertive means:

- Balancing your feelings, words, and behaviors to establish healthy boundaries, but also convey trust.

- Speaking your mind in a way that showcases sturdy confidence but also friendly flexibility. (You do this by reviewing your belief system, defining things you are and aren't willing to tolerate, and ultimately, assuming responsibility for your thoughts, feelings, and actions.)

- Developing emotional awareness of your inner thoughts, ambitions, and desires and identifying your core strengths and weaknesses.

Personal Development Mastery

Learning how to process negative feelings and overcome personal limitations by reviewing how you thought, felt, and reacted in successful situations to apply these patterns to situations you find challenging.

Personal Development Mastery

Chapter 8: Being a Charismatic Leader

How to Motivate Others to Be Excited About Doing What You Persuade Them to Do

Throughout the previous chapters of this book, we defined and emphasized the importance of possessing and exuding charisma to advance in all areas of life. As you learned, charisma is a trait nurtured through devotion to yourself and your core value system. It manifests in your awareness of what you stand for and expressing it with your body language, facial expressions, speech, actions, and appearance. For someone who is yet to start your journey, this is easier said than done. Of course, if living and acting on your best intentions were so easy, everyone would be doing it.

Without a doubt, journeying through life will require

overcoming obstacles. Some of them are more obvious (e.g., gaining skills and competencies, getting to know people, and building your reputation). However, being at the very top of the ladder (a spot reserved for those who not only play roles in society but also build and grow companies and organizations and work to make a difference in the world) takes overcoming one more obstacle: learning how to influence others.

You see, your heart may be in the right place, and what you stand up for may make complete sense in your mind (and perhaps even in the minds of others). However, when you're working on spreading new messages and sharing original ideas, one of your tasks will be to persuade others to join in. There's a chance that individuals and groups who play an important role in the fulfillment of your mission may not see things the way you do, so you'll have to give them a nudge. Say you want to start a charity. You'll have to persuade people that your plan has a true impact on society. Or, if you're applying for a business loan, you'll have to convince the decision-makers that your business plan truly has a chance of success. For this, you'll need to develop the skill to influence.

Now, if your heart is in the right place (as it is the case with most people), there's a chance that you think that influencing is the same as manipulation. But what if it's not? If you think about it, "manipulating" means to give a false presentation of yourself and to use other people for personal gain. Manipulation is harmful to those who are being used, while influence isn't.

The key difference between manipulation and influence is that being influential doesn't abuse people's weaknesses and insecurities. Instead, it means wielding the power that comes from your integrity and confidence to convey a message people will believe. But it won't be because they're being lied to but because they trust your judgment and put their faith in your abilities. Much like the people you're aiming to influence, you too are being influenced every day. Either consciously or subconsciously, your decisions and actions are based on the trust in judgment and opinions of those you find trustworthy—whether it's your spouse, family, doctor, teacher, or a politician. So why wouldn't you be one of those people, and more importantly, how do you become one?

Being a charismatic leader means becoming a figure of influence. A charismatic leader, as research found, is someone who has a strong presence. On the other hand, being pleasant in appearance and approachable is a part of affability, which is the second key characteristic of charismatic leaders. As it turns out, people are very good at evaluating their level of charisma. Research also shows that if you were to rate how charismatic you are on a scale of 1–5, you would probably be right.

Before we delve further into this chapter, I'd like you to pause for a second and rate your level of charisma. Now, it's time to compare where you are now with the level you want to be at. If you don't think of yourself as being as charismatic as you'd like, there's also a good chance you know the reasons for that. What are the leadership traits and qualities you want to work on? If you're unsure which of the key skills and competencies need additional boosting, this chapter will present you with some traits and skills you can work on.

The key influences to develop if you want to become a charismatic leader are presence, leadership skills, and affability. This list may be short, but it encompasses a wide range of personal strengths, skills, and competencies to develop first.

Presence

Having a strong presence is the number-one trait of charismatic leaders. However, this trait encompasses four different characteristics to develop: confidence, self-esteem, optimism, and resilience. You see, as a leader, you will get all the perks of being influential. You'll get the spotlight and the power to make decisions, which will manifest in money, assets, and quality personal relationships. But with great powers come great responsibilities. You'll need to have the courage to step out first and fight for your goal, make plans, decide the right course of action, and accept the responsibility for risks and failures. This will take knowing how to predict and overcome obstacles and knowing how to solve problems.

Now perhaps it's a bit clearer why only a handful of

people dare to lead. First, it takes a considerable amount of confidence to carry out this role. You need other people to believe that you can do the things you set out to do, and you need to believe that you're able to do them. Many people are good at convincing others, but not so much themselves. This is why indecisiveness, risky actions, and ineffective ones take place.

Your effectiveness and power as a charismatic leader grow with confidence and faith in your abilities. Your confidence, on the other hand, will grow with the ability to communicate across a variety of settings, groups, and individuals. Public speaking is perhaps the biggest challenge for one's confidence, and practicing it surely benefits your growth.

Aside from being confident, charismatic people are also optimistic. It shouldn't be difficult to understand why people want to follow those who built them up and not those who beat them down. So ask yourself which effect you think your presence has on the people around you. People are very good at detecting superficial, false optimism. Your task will be to nurture a genuinely positive outlook on everyday situations, even the challenging ones.

Being genuinely positive means making an effort to see the best in different situations, events, and people. However, to act in this way in all cases takes developing a good emotional compass and knowing what kind of positive outlook is appropriate for the moment. Let's say you're attending a meeting during which you found out that the organization needs to fire a certain amount of people. What's the right measure of optimism to use here? Surely, this is not the time to be overly cheerful. Instead, you can frame the situation as temporarily ending working relationships for the sake of long-term stability.

If you were the one to fire those people, what would be an appropriate thing to tell them? Remember, many of these people need consolation and encouragement. Many of these people would lose their jobs with loans and mortgages to pay or sick family members to support. If you were to practice charismatic leadership in this situation, what would you do? Undoubtedly, assuring those being let go that their skills, talents, and contribution will always be appreciated is the first step. It also helps to share a couple of supportive sentences about the direction they could take to grow their career going forward.

These would be genuine expressions of optimism in potentially defeating situations. How you leave things with people around you undoubtedly sets the tone for how you'll be seen in the eyes of those who you depend on. The fruits of being empathetic won't fail to show.

In the long run, positive communication helps you establish yourself as someone trustworthy and capable of managing problems, all while taking care of those who depend on you. This allows people around you to feel more optimistic, and you want that, whether they're above or below your rank. This is because those who are below you can push you up, and those who are above you can give a helping hand so that you reach the next level.

Both positive thinking and a positive outlook on events taking place, as you can see, create powerful tools in solving problems and negotiating solutions, whether it's at work or home.

While you can use your influence for both positive and negative purposes, keep in mind that the former yields lasting betterment for yourself and others in the long run, while the latter only has temporary benefits. The most powerful type of influence is the one that unites people around a common cause, and personal progress and benefits become only the side effects of it.

Leadership Skills

People with strong leadership skills grow and nurture them actively and on purpose, although it may seem that their charisma is God-given. Leadership is a matter of intent, decision, and action—first on self-improvement and then on fulfilling your mission and goals. Successful leaders use different leadership styles, all developed with hard work. These competencies help them convey their vision and messages in different settings and to different people, tailored around the circumstances and individual traits of those they lead. This is done using strong communication skills.

Affability

Developing the skill of conveying an attractive, inviting presence that inspires people to talk to you, engage in your plans, and listen to what you have to say is the third most important leadership quality. If you think of any leader you respect (be it Tony Robbins, Oprah Winfrey, or even Aragorn from the *Lord of the Rings*), what do you see these people having in common? They make you feel good about yourself, and they make you feel even better about yourself when you imagine being in their presence. You want to talk to them, confide in them, share your biggest fears and insecurities, and ask for their guidance on what to do to solve your problems. All of these individuals are affable. They all make people feel good and comfortable. But how do you develop this ability?

The best way to become affable is to work on growing your emotional intelligence. Tuning your emotional radar will help you understand people's feelings, motives, and actions better. It teaches you how to speak to them and share your message.

Another important part of being affable is being optimistic, which we thoroughly discussed in the previous section. But to have an optimistic outlook also requires knowing how to command your feelings so that your behavior doesn't come across as exaggerated or superficial. It will help you appeal to the best in other people so that you can direct the relationship toward what you want to achieve.

Aside from this, charismatic people are good at knowing when to show and when to hide their feelings. Of course, acting the way you feel isn't suitable or effective in all situations. In many of them, it can be quite harmful. Powerful leaders maintain a unique serene exterior, with the hustle and the work needed in growing their vision hidden from sight. This isn't lying, as it may appear. Acting in this way allows other people to focus on the essence of what you're trying to say. It helps to emphasize your key message.

Say you want to inspire people to follow your training program. Do they need to know you're struggling financially because of your student loan? Not really. Nowhere in your job description does it say they do or that it affects your credibility. So why would they have known about how you hustled to secure the funds for starting your business? Rest assured, they only want to see your rock-solid muscles and hear all about how to grow them with your assistance.

How to Quickly Read Anyone and Know What Triggers Will Influence Them

Being interesting to other people is another common trait of approachable leaders. A polished look and a smile on your face make you charming. The same is true when you have listening, communication, and storytelling skills and use appropriate optimism and humor. People want to be around interesting people. To grow this trait, pay attention to people's feedback. What are the most appealing parts of your interaction with them? Whether it is a public performance or a networking event, hearing people's impressions is useful to find out which of your skills are the strongest and which need some boosting.

How to Become Influential

Aside from the traits already mentioned (i.e., confidence, optimism, listening skills, and communication skills), here are a couple more skills to develop to become attractive to other people:

1. Passion and drive: Being passionate about the things you love and the job you do is inspiring. It draws people to you, as it appeals to their inner drive and passions. Being passionate gives meaning to mundane, everyday tasks, and being the one to remind people of that makes you a person they look up to.

2. Courage: Leadership means handling gigantic responsibilities, evaluating and making business deals, making bold decisions, and taking risks for the sake of everyone's personal growth and the fulfillment of the common goal. Learning how to be bold and brave means nurturing confidence and resilience to frustration, stress, fear, and failure.

3. Humor: The ability to make people laugh conveys

confidence, but it also helps other people stay optimistic in the face of challenges. Learning how to use appropriate humor by analyzing the work of other leaders you admire, as well as your favorite comedians, will help establish yourself as a person people can turn to when they feel discouraged and need a confidence boost.

Now that you know why it is important to be charismatic, let's start practicing it, shall we?

As mentioned earlier, there are good chances that you can accurately evaluate how charismatic you are. If you're not completely happy with your result, you can start practicing some of the techniques to nurture personal charisma. The fact is that you can significantly grow your personal magnetism in a matter of weeks if you only practice daily and consistently. There are particular steps you can take to notice an improvement in less than a month!

Without further ado, here are the strategies to become more charismatic:

1. Let your inner self shine through your outfit. Whether it's business attire, casual chic, or romantic flare, your style can do a great service to help you communicate your inner self. Before anything else, people around you will notice your outfit. The best part is that you can dress into suitable, stylish, and original outfits on any budget. However, the main rule is to only wear those items that spark joy. Whichever piece of clothing you put on, make sure it makes you feel happy and comfortable. Discomfort hurts charisma because people can spot that you feel uncomfortable.

2. *Practice eye contact.* Finding a good measure of pleasant, genuine, and appropriate eye contact will take exercise. To learn how to make impactful eye contact, hold it only a second longer than usual. The ultimate achievement is to maintain eye contact until the other person looks away. It might seem a bit strange at the beginning, but the more you practice, the more you'll build a habit of maintaining natural eye contact throughout the majority of the conversation. Only look away and break contact for purposes of thinking about what the other person is saying, pointing to an item used in the conversation, or taking a pause when speaking. These little natural breaks will help the eye contact stay consistent but not creepy.

3. *Stand your ground.* The art of assertiveness and charisma is all about making your presence known. For this, you'll have to learn a little bit about maintaining your territory, which subtly yet effectively signals personal power. You will start by taking slightly more space as you walk. Observe your stance as you walk the streets or enter a room. Do you shrug your shoulders and bow your head, mentally trying to make yourself invisible? Not anymore. Lift your head, straighten your shoulders, and spread your arms as much as possible while walking to feel more powerful but still natural. If you want to measure the ideal position, have your hands parallel with your shoulders, a few inches from your thighs, but with the elbows pointed outwards. As you walk, let your left-hand wave forward with the right leg and the other way around. This type of walk will help you feel and come across as stronger.

4. Set your boundaries. Boundaries are difficult for many people, but most notable at work. This is because the workplace is an environment with more people to push them. While some people are good at setting boundaries at work, many are less successful in personal life, where they can't say no to friends and family. Either way, setting boundaries requires making it clear what you will and will not tolerate. Your job is to sit down and review what you won't tolerate from people around you. Determining your boundaries means deciding what's acceptable and what's not, and it's okay to have different standards for home and work, as well as for different people. Now, to practice setting boundaries, you also need to start making them clear. Learn how to voice your boundaries assertively. Make sure that your response is balanced with the situation and that you're stating a clear message without overreacting.

Summary

In this chapter, you learned how to develop the qualities that make a charismatic leader. You learned that persuasion isn't the same as manipulation. While manipulation preys on people's insecurities to abuse them for personal gain, persuasion resides on the art of convincing others to accept your point of view. To become persuasive and influential, you'll need to grow specific skills and qualities, including the following:

- *Presence and affability:* Presence means nurturing your sense of purpose and displaying it in your appearance, interactions, and actions. Affability, on the other hand, is a quality that combines friendliness, personal appeal, and relatability. To build this quality, you have to get to know people from all walks of life and learn to talk to those who have different tastes, opinions, and values than yours.

Learning how to read people to get what you want: This may appear as manipulation, but it can't be further from the truth. Reading people means finding ways to speak your message so that they understand it within their value system.

Chapter 9: Group Interactions

Communication is a widely researched scientific field and particularly well-studied in the area of leadership. It's no wonder since leadership mainly consists of communicating ideas, plans, messages, intentions, and motivation. As it turns out, successful leaders have powerful communication skills. They are able to appeal to people's most intimate emotions, send messages without causing conflict, and resolve disputes by sending the right messages. But how do they do that?

Communicating in group settings can become complex because you're working with a variety of different personalities, backgrounds, cultures, and individual character traits. For this reason, leaders tend to develop communication styles that are authentic to them but suitable to environments and individuals they work with. They understand that, aside from information, interactions also depend on beliefs, intentions, and motivation. They are capable of understanding why people say the things they're saying and why they act the way they do.

Group Interaction Skills for Charismatic Leaders

While there are many things that distinguish leaders and many situations that typically result in leader emergence, *communication*, *competence*, and *skill* are the primary traits that create the conditions for one to become a leader. Leadership studies that focus solely on communication skills reveal that people with above-average communication talent may emerge as leaders even when they're not in a leadership role. People with enhanced leadership skills are good at balancing personal relationships with tasks and procedures in a group setting. Typically, a person who understands and facilitates the dynamic of the group toward the common goal may emerge or be chosen as a leader. Below is a list of things that a good leader does.

1. They contribute ideas.

Good communicators make good leaders because they know how to *give, ask for, and interpret information accurately.* For leadership to be productive and beneficial for everyone involved, it's important for leaders to offer as many ideas as needed. This is because contributing puts them in a position of being evaluated by their group members, which strengthens the group dynamic. Whenever you're participating in group work, research shows that a simple way to grow your communication skills is to switch perspectives. On the one hand, give honest but constructive opinions about other people's contributions and ideas. On the other hand, participate with the same amount of ideas so that you, too, can get feedback on your work.

2. They contribute to group functions.

Now, from an interaction stance, leaders must contribute to group functions to be beneficial to the group. They should *seek, evaluate, and provide ideas but also ask others to evaluate their ideas.* They should be able to visualize abstract concepts and generalize concepts and patterns across different ideas and fields. These behaviors help the group work toward the common goal and become more successful overall. Still, most people have preferences when it comes to tasks they prefer doing, and they are more successful in some of them than others. Despite their abilities, leaders should still delegate and turn over certain tasks to other group members.

3. They do their best to achieve their goals.

Your interaction skills should include communication skills that are relevant for the group cause or its functioning. More specifically, you should be able to identify and *set goals, create reasonable plans for their completion, and be able to summarize and clarify all the complex tasks and procedures* so that the group remains focused on specific tasks. Group leaders are also good at creating an inclusive culture, and they help establish norms for how the members will value individual and group work. They create an encouraging, supportive, safe environment without criticism.

4. They guide intergroup communication.

Growing your communication skills will require guiding the communication process in your group. By contributing *creative ideas for how your group can communicate better,* you can establish yourself as someone who understands the group dynamic and can help the entire team communicate effectively. This way, you may contribute to resolving conflicts and help the group function better going forward. For this, you should nurture the following traits of group interaction: regulating participation, helping people evaluate their contributions, conflict solving, and assessing group climate.

5. They develop public speaking skills.

Not only public speaking but also successful group speaking is a part of every leader's communication skills. While public speaking may be intimidating, it comes with a significant advantage: you're the center of attention, and no one can interrupt you. When you're speaking to a group of listeners, you're free to express your message undisturbed. But when you're working with a group and your goal is to navigate the course of a conversation, your communication skills can be put to the test. Whichever type of interaction it is, you'll have to learn to overcome shyness first.

6. They face challenging people.

Speaking to different people is in every leader's daily itinerary. It should become a habit and something you do well spontaneously and effortlessly. Interaction requires and strengthens confidence. Regardless of how confident you feel, in the beginning, learning to talk to different people will only help you feel better about yourself.

The more you talk to people, the better you'll understand how your speaking and listening skills, body language, and presence play a role in daily interactions and how all of this changes the quality of your life. The more you talk, the better you'll notice how problems get solved faster, how willing people are to help out, and how you come across in the eyes of your observers.

However, to master these skills, you shouldn't only talk to people you get along with. Instead, practice talking to people of all ages, genders, professions, and interests. This will help you learn how different personality profiles think, speak, and act. It's particularly important not to shy away from people who are challenging your confidence, whether it is because of a different relationship or because they intimidate you with their appearance. A lot of times, even people we admire can make us shy. This can be someone you respect or look up to (e.g., your favorite teacher or your boss) or even someone you like (e.g., your crush). Whoever these people are, overcoming shyness when talking to them helps you get to know them better, understand where they come from, and build your confidence.

As you get used to talking to new people each day, you can try having longer, deeper, and more meaningful conversations. This is important to build your presence. You might think that popular people are those who never approach others but instantly become the center of attention. You couldn't be more wrong! Most people who have a presence show initiative to get to know other people, and they approach them first. As you practice approaching people, you'll also learn how friendlier people act when someone gives them positive attention. This will help you feel more connected with the people around you and increase your social circle. It will also make it easier to take the initiative and become more proactive.

7. They learn and stay informed.

Another way to boost your confidence when speaking with people is to beat insecurities with education. Your insecurities and nervousness could stem from a lack of knowledge, whether it is about the conversation topic or social skills in general. If you feel socially unequipped in any way (e.g., you don't know what's the most appropriate thing to say or which gestures are natural and suitable for the occasion), the best way to become more confident is to write down the reasons behind your anxiety and insecurity and then read and learn about the particular topics.

Sadly, many educated, talented experts never get to showcase their knowledge and skills in their best light. This is mainly because insecurity gets in the way of speaking. To overcome this, make sure to do some research before making important social contacts. At times, it would be about the conversation itself and other times about people you'll engage with or the type of interaction (e.g., a meeting, a party, a date, or a networking event).

The third thing you can do to stop being shy and withdrawn is to be active and engaged in conversations. No amount of reading and learning can compensate for practice, and the same goes for developing speaking skills as well. The more you talk to people, the more you'll practice your skills and become more socially competent. As time passes, you'll get used to interacting and be able to focus more on how to present yourself and share strong messages.

Summary

In this chapter, you learned that all leaders have well-developed group interaction skills. Below are some tips that can help you develop these skills:

- *Share ideas and insights, and contribute to the group in that way.* When your team receives suggestions from you, they will see you as a part of the group rather than someone who only manages the work.

- *Contribute to group functioning by focusing on the goals and tasks the group is ought to fulfill.* The best way to learn how to communicate with a group is to get to know its dynamics. Plain and simple, think of what the group is about. Who are its members? What's their character and expertise profile? More importantly, what can you do so that the group does its job better?

- *Focus on group goals.* People will follow a leader who takes them to a place where they want to be. If it's a work group, the goal will depend on projects, tasks, and strategic goals. In informal groups, it will be education or entertainment. Either way, your performance, competence, and significance will be judged by how well you guide people to do or get the thing they came for.

- *Guide group communication.* Want to be a leader? Lead the group talk. Help people clarify their messages. Understand other members properly. Resolve their conflicts. In other words, be a mediator (more on that in the next chapter). Remember, a leader is a person whom people can rely on to look at the big picture while they focus on smaller, more manageable tasks.

- *Master public speaking.* Shyness and insecurity are normal for every person, but a leader must learn to overcome them. Focus on the messages you're trying to pass and back them up with strong body language, aside from working on your speaking skills.
- *Talk to people who test your values, beliefs, tastes, and preferences.* Only by facing those you disagree with while staying respectful will your messages hold merit. Aside from that, talking to diverse personalities will help you understand how people from different walks of life think and feel. You will also learn how to adjust your style and communication for your message to be heard accurately.
- *Learn about communication, leadership, your profession, and all other fields of interest.* People

always want to learn something new and interesting. Being eloquent and well-informed, as well as knowing how to wrap it up in an appealing exterior and expression, will position you in other people's eyes as someone who is a valuable resource of knowledge and inspiration.

You're almost there! You got through 9 out of 10 essential steps to becoming a charismatic leader! In the first chapter, you learned how to navigate intergroup communication. But what happens when things get rough? Despite your best effort, there's always a chance of conflict. A conflict can occur either between you and someone else or between other members of your group. Your role as a leader will be to solve it. In the next chapter, you'll find out how to work through individual and group conflicts to contribute to mutual goals and mutual growth.

Chapter 10: Handling Conflicts

Conflicts occur naturally both in workplaces and personal life. Generally speaking, conflict is a collision of contrasting ideas, opinions, interests, or views on the same situation. As someone who strives toward being a leader, unity is one of the key values to represent, and unity will require knowing how to resolve conflicts. In this chapter, you'll learn what conflicts are, how they occur, and how to overcome or work around them.

Types of Conflict and the Best Ways to Find a Solution

Good leaders are good at solving conflicts. A conflict can occur in any group of people and for a multitude of reasons. Conflict occurs when people don't interact. They are signs that the relationships and communication in a group need some work. Wise leaders can use group conflict to open up opportunities for improvement and to move closer toward the common goal. If not, conflicts have the potential to cause many adverse business-related and personal outcomes. If you want to improve your conflict management skills, you'll need to start learning how to create a productive work environment. It is an atmosphere of mutual help, collaboration, and learning. In any group, members will work better when they work together.

Why Conflict Occurs?

Conflicts can happen for various reasons—e.g., differences in opinion to feelings, cultures, religion, attitude, looks, race, or gender. Conflicting positions, roles, statuses, and values can also cause conflicts. A conflict can also be a blend of different causes. Regardless of the cause, a good leader understands that conflict is a normal part of life. They expect it to happen and know how to manage it. While it is unpleasant, conflict is a necessary experience that helps people evaluate actions, decisions, and consequences of their choices so that they can have better ways to move forward.

However, people often avoid conflict as it can result in unpleasant feelings. Conflict can make people feel angry, afraid, ashamed, or guilty, which is why many people are prone to suppressing it. If well-managed, conflict can still contribute to the betterment of work environments. Research shows that there's a great chance that people will feel like they understand each other better, improve their working relationships, become more skillful in finding solutions, perform better, and become more motivated to do productive work if they are in an environment that's good with managing conflict. This way, leadership skills that boost workplace productivity don't only increase your personal influence but also benefit the entire organization.

Conflict can occur on multiple levels—e.g., between people, within oneself, and in and between groups.

Between people: Interpersonal conflict can happen between individuals with opposing goals or different approaches to their relationship. Different personality types can create differences in opinions and choices. When conflicts like these occur, it's necessary to compromise. Unaddressed personal conflict, if suppressed, can culminate in the inability to communicate.

With oneself: Intrapersonal conflict is the type of conflict that happens in the mind of a person. A person can have mutually conflicting thoughts, wishes, principles, and feelings. Unless addressed, these conflicts can also lead to anxiety and depression. Intrapersonal conflicts may affect other relationships as well, creating interpersonal conflicts. Talking to trusted friends and coworkers is usually the best way to resolve these conflicts because it helps you weigh your options and circumstances to make the best decision.

In and between groups: Conflict can happen within and

between groups. When there are divisions in a group or when there are conflicting views, opinions, and values, it can create friction and a competitive environment. These situations can escalate as well and become very destructive. Usually, intergroup conflicts can have great costs, but they can also yield great progress with proper management. Conflicts within members of the same group can arise due to differences in personalities, unclear roles, differences in workload, and other factors. But how does a good leader manage conflicts successfully?

Best Ways to Manage a Conflict

Collaboration and compromise are the two most successful ways of managing conflicts. Both of these strategies contribute to group progress and growth.

Collaboration usually takes a lot of time and energy because it's necessary to establish all the needs and goals involved with the conflict. This way, the leader can facilitate the resolution by discovering ideas that can create positive outcomes for everyone affected. Here, it's also important to identify those feelings that intervene with group dynamics. However, it may not be suitable in situations where a quick and effective decision must be made.

Compromise is another conflict-solving strategy that helps reach common ground. With compromise, both parties are partially satisfied. Neither of the parties wins or loses; instead, they get an acceptable solution. Usually, reaching a satisfactory solution is possible when two sides split differences, trade concerns, or find a middle ground. However, compromise can sometimes lead to manipulation and perception of unfairness. Compromise is the best approach for both parties when other solutions don't seem to work or when there's too little to gain and too much to lose for either of the parties.

Conflict-Solving in Leadership

Knowing how to resolve conflicts successfully distinguishes true leaders from those who only strive to be leaders. Unlike those who see conflicts as problems, leaders see them as an opportunity to introduce positive changes. One of the most admirable leadership qualities is knowing what to say and how to respond during conflicts. Those who avoid confrontation tend to allow tensions in the workplace to build up, which has devastating consequences on work climate and productivity. Here are a couple of examples of how leaders step up to resolve conflicts and get people on their side:

1. Validate feelings. When people come to you feeling frustrated or angry, it's usually because they've been experiencing something stressful for a while. On top of that, they could fear speaking their mind will make the situation worse. Successful leaders never ignore people's feelings. Instead, they accept and recognize the significance of these feelings and express empathy, which helps reduce tension.

2. Suggest a break. When a leader senses that someone (either them or the other person) isn't capable of talking rationally, they suggest taking a break before allowing the conflict to get worse. Taking a couple of deep breaths helps people see if they've exaggerated, and it also helps them pinpoint the exact point of the problem, instead of blaming their team, work, or the entire organization. Office negotiations can get heated, and depending on the industry, a lot can be at stake from making one over another decision. In situations like these, leaders help the members of their team understand how the actions of everyone involved affect the end goal, making the argument less personal.

3. Praise feedback. A lot of the time, people are afraid of coming up to say that something bothers them, whether it's a coworker or a boss. Doing this can be even more difficult in environments that emphasize positivity and creativity. Here, employees may start to feel as if they're being toxic or hostile by pointing out that there's something wrong with how the company handles their business. However, this can have negative long-term effects on productivity. When employees are not happy, the quality of work is affected, talented workers walk away, and productivity suffers. Instead, make sure your coworkers know that you value their feedback even when you don't agree. This will help them feel acknowledged, and at the same time, show that coming straight to you to solve problems pays off. On the other hand, even if you end up turning down another person's request, appreciating their feedback will make them feel better, and they are more likely to understand the rationale behind your answer.

4. Praise effort. Most of the time, it is the result that receives the most appreciation. But some contributions can't be measured by figures—e.g., a person's loyalty or engagement in projects that fell through. Don't forget to mention and praise these invisible contributions. When people feel acknowledged and appreciated, they're more likely to work hard and be productive than when they feel like the result is all that matters. It is particularly important to give credit to everyone involved in a project because it's not uncommon for only a couple of individuals to take credit for a result that took the entire team's devoted work. This is profoundly discouraging to talented employees who will start to question whether they will ever receive the acknowledgment for their contributions.

5. Work together. Motivating people to work together to solve a problem helps establish a partnership in the office rather than passing the blame. When people are encouraged to work as partners, they're more likely to assume responsibility for their actions. When people are made to feel like there must be a winner and a loser, they're a lot less likely to cooperate. In a competitive environment, people can start feeling like taking responsibility for their mistakes means they'll be seen as a failure, while the other person wins. This is very toxic and can get in the way of a healthy working climate.

How to Resolve Personal Conflicts to Sway People on Your Side

There are many ways for you to handle conflict as a charismatic leader. Many of these are applicable across a wide range of settings and situations. Whichever you choose, keep in mind that the very choice to face a conflict instead of avoiding confrontation makes a world of difference. While finding common ground might take some extra effort, people won't fail to notice that you are helping make the workplace a better, more pleasant space for them. Indeed, resolving conflict requires a careful approach, but it is always better than trying to pretend like it is not there.

When conflict solving is promoted in the entire organization, people no longer see conflicts as something dramatic. Instead, the entire team and staff members know how to cope with them, and they are capable of finding a solution that will be acceptable to everyone. However, to manage conflict well, you need to be familiar with the entire working system. First, you have to evaluate the consequences of people's actions. To understand how each of the participants contributed to the conflict, you'll have to understand the office climate, their process, and structure first. But, what if you find yourself in a direct conflict despite doing your best to communicate and work in harmony? Here are the crucial steps for winning in this situation:

1. Ask for more information. There's nothing more appealing in the workplace than a superior who truly wants to find out what people think about their work, whether or not something bothers them, or if there's an issue they need help with. Wanting to know people's concerns shows them that you're genuinely interested in your employees. When people feel valued and heard, it reduces tensions and helps maintain a more tolerant work environment. On the other hand, when they feel like the organization or the management doesn't care for their concerns, they're more likely to be less productive.

2. Prevent mistakes from repeating. As a leader of a business or the organization, you'll frequently experience different errors or issues. When this happens, it's extremely important not to pass the blame but instead do everything you can for the mistake and the negative consequences that resulted from it not to happen ever again. When you do this, people lose their defensive attitude and become more solution-oriented. On the other hand, when you insert yourself into finding a solution, you show them that there's equality in solving problems rather than a chain of command.

3. Find something to agree on. Acknowledging at least one point about which the other person is right helps them feel validated. When a person feels like they are being heard instead of being dismissed, they'll be more likely to participate in solving a problem. Being dismissive of other people's opinions only increases tension and anger, which further prevents resolving a conflict or finding a solution for a difficult situation.

4. Don't act like you know everything. Good leaders aren't afraid to show that they aren't familiar with something, and they demonstrate a desire to learn and hear more. These leaders get to see how a situation looks like from another person's point of view. Even if you think you know everything about a particular problem, there's always a chance that there are details you aren't aware of, but you would want to know. The more you ask questions and listen, the better you'll be able to understand the issue and find out what you can do to solve it.

5. Hold yourself accountable. Most people feel like the only way to win respect and credibility is to always be right, which is simply not possible. Instead, express accountability when you are being called out for a certain behavior. Being defensive isn't at all recommended in these situations because it takes a lot to win people over, but it's very easy to lose them. Keep in mind that people are coming to you with complaints they already believe to be the truth, and they count on their accusations being denied. If you justify their expectations, you will establish yourself as someone whose ego doesn't allow them to improve.

6. Offer support. Leaders who offer support, whether it's in casual conversation or during problem-solving, get to hear about the problems their associates, team members, or employees have. When you ask someone about how you can provide help and support, you make them feel acknowledged and safe, which can defuse conflicts and help people become more patient. This is particularly important in complex situations where it's not easy to establish who is responsible for a particular mistake or when people are unable to find common ground.

Being responsible when resolving conflicts will earn your respect among peers and employees. Your job isn't to be popular but efficient. When you're able to "put your money where your mouth is" and show people on your team what you're capable of, your popularity and credibility will grow. However, solving conflicts is essential here because conflicts affect the quality of work. Showing that you have problem-solving skills helps everyone trust your ability to resolve other problems as well.

Often, leaders try to create a harmonious, pleasant work environment artificially. This means that they avoid confronting tensions but instead create a toxic environment for their employees. Essentially, problems are being swept under the rug. When things like these happen, people involved in the business lose trust in those they should look up to, and they start seeing them as shallow and greedy. How do you avoid this?

Using the aforementioned tools, you need to intervene right away. Perhaps you don't feel like you know enough to face an issue, and it could be true. Because of that, you should take a couple of days and talk to people to get to the bottom of a conflict. The more you do this; the more your associates will feel like you're taking their problems seriously. The work won't suffer as well because now that everyone in charge found a way to cope with their frustrations, they can start working productively again.

<u>Summary</u>

You've now taken the final step toward becoming a charismatic leader. In this chapter, you learned the following:

- Conflict naturally occurs between people, whether it's in the workplace or in your personal life. While the conflict occurrence itself isn't something to worry about, it shows that there's a lack of effective communication.

- Conflict can take place between people, in a group, between groups, and even within a single person. Causes for conflict can be differences of opinion, conflicting interests, and other issues that call for the use of collaboration and compromise as a way of finding a resolution.

- Collaboration means getting people to work together to find a solution. While it is the best way to resolve conflict, it's not always possible. Often, people don't want to give up on some of their interests and motivations for the sake of achieving the common goal. In this case, compromise is the ultimate solution.

- Compromise means finding a middle ground. It is a solution in which all parties involved both win and lose something for the sake of achieving the goal. As a leader, you should compromise rather than use your power and influence to win. While it is possible to get what you want by using personal power, there's a risk of compromising your reputation.

Personal Development Mastery

Conclusion

Congratulations! You've made it to the end of your manual for becoming a charismatic leader. Now, you know the necessary skills you need to develop personal, financial, and business success.

The purpose of this book was to show you how you can beat shyness and anxiety to become a charismatic leader whom people will want to follow. We covered the essential talents and skills you need to develop for magnetic personal charisma.

For this, you first learned how to make a memorable first impression. As you discovered, first impressions are hard to shake away. People carry them around as an unconscious evaluation of your character no matter what you do afterward. In this book, you learned that to make a good first impression, you first need to adopt a confident, positive attitude. You learned that you need to be dressed to impress, and you need to exude confidence so that people remember your staple inner strength.

After that, you learned not only how to showcase confidence but also how to nurture it so that it's genuine and rock-solid. You learned the basic steps for training confidence. In particular, you learned how important it is to pay attention to your health, appearance, skills, knowledge, and values. You learned that being well-prepared for the occasion helps you beat shyness, nervousness, and insecurity. With this knowledge, you can proceed to share the best of your abilities with the world and no longer hide behind the fear that someone will judge you.

After that, you learned how to adopt a leadership mindset by becoming a good listener, remembering people's names, and making small talk like a true pro you are. You learned that, sadly, your positive traits, knowledge, and skills don't speak for themselves. Instead, you need to know how to present yourself to remain memorable and recognizable. To do this, you need to sport a polished appearance, listen carefully, and engage in casual conversations.

However, this is often easier said than done. As you learned in the second chapter of this book, there's a reason why so many people struggle with being memorable. It's called low confidence, coupled with a lack of self-esteem and often an equally poor self-image. As you learned, one must think positively of themselves and eliminate all self-doubt to nurture true charisma. In this book, you were given tools to nurture your sense of personal value and start improving your self-image. With the tools and exercises offered in this book, you can begin analyzing your biggest personal strengths and truly appreciating yourself for who you are unconditionally and without any doubt.

As you learned the importance of being confident, you also learned the value of building key leadership skills. First things first—you learned how to be a good listener by paying attention, processing, and responding to what another person is saying. These skills, while perhaps challenging to develop, will be put to good use the further you delve into building up your presence and making yourself noticeable.

Being a leader, as you learned, requires a reciprocal exchange of listening, speaking, ideas, and feedback. For one to become a leader, one must inspire. They must establish themselves as an authority figure but also a figure of trust and support. To build yourself up to that level, you need to possess the ability of captivating storytelling, interacting with groups, and solving conflicts.

To make a good first impression now seems easy, doesn't it? After the initial steps, the time came for you to learn how to inspire, entertain, and teach with your stories. You learned how to become a skillful mediator so that you can resolve your own conflicts and those within your team.

As you learned, for one to achieve their goal, they must

know how to make other people work toward that goal. And what better way to do it than to understand and support their goals and motivations so that they reciprocate with actions needed for your progress? But on that path, obstacles may arise. You learned how to use your communication skills and body language to convey trust, capability, and confidence. But what if that's not enough?

Oftentimes, conflicts and heated arguments occur despite your best effort. Whether it's helping your team resolve their disputes or trying to work out a solution in a personal conflict, you found out how important it is to listen, appreciate feedback, praise contributions, and work toward finding common ground. You learned that, while there are obscure ways to manipulate people, the path that leads to continual growth is the one of understanding, collaboration, and compromise. As you learned, these ways of resolving conflicts depend on the degree to which people can align their goals and intentions. More importantly, you learned all the tips and tricks needed for detecting the invisible and navigating it to your advantage.

As you reach the final lines of this book, I want to leave you with a final message to not waste a second before you start exploring your authenticity. This is done through self-awareness and learning how to observe and analyze not only your goals and intentions but also your true capabilities. Once you realize where your true talents lie, you have found the exact strengths and valuable resources to share with the world. Your talents, skills, passions, and positive values are your most prized possession. They hold the key to dressing, speaking, acting, and leading in a way that works for what you discover to be your life's true purpose.

Your purpose, which is unique and infinitely valuable, is what makes you a leader. It is your mission to complete, a battle to fight for, and a legacy to preserve. It is the spark beneath your shine and the force behind the magnetic appeal you'll possess after you've looked inside. Stay authentic, and good luck in fulfilling your noble mission of leading those who are willing to follow!

Personal Development Mastery

Get My New Books For FREE!

I love writing about personal development, and I am constantly in the trenches of writing a new book.

If you want to receive a **FREE COPY** of any future books I am releasing, please sign up to my free **VIP List** to receive your **FREE COPY**.

Sign up at:

https://bit.ly/RichardBanksVIP

Thank you for reading!

REFERENCES

Berry, D. S., & Hansen, J. S. (1996). Positive affect, negative affect, and social interaction. *Journal of personality and social psychology*, 71(4), 796. https://psycnet.apa.org/doi/10.1037/0022-3514.71.4.796

Cohen, G. (1990). Why is it difficult to put names to faces?. *British Journal of Psychology*, 81(3), 287–297. https://doi.org/10.1111/j.2044-8295.1990.tb02362.x

Diener, E., & Seligman, M. E. (2002). Very happy people. *Psychological science*, 13(1), 81-84. https://doi.org/10.1111%2F1467-9280.00415

Griffin, M. A., Neal, A., & Parker, S. K. (2007). A new model of work role performance: Positive behavior in uncertain and interdependent contexts. *Academy of management journal*, 50(2), 327–347. https://doi.org/10.5465/amj.2007.24634438

Klich, N. R., & Feldman, D. C. (1992). The role of approval and achievement needs in feedback seeking behavior. *Journal of Managerial Issues*, 554–570.

Mayo, M., Kakarika, M., Pastor, J. C., & Brutus, S. (2012). Aligning or inflating your leadership self-image? A longitudinal study of responses to peer feedback in MBA teams. *Academy of Management Learning & Education*, 11(4), 631–652. https://doi.org/10.5465/amle.2010.0069

Neck, C. P., & Manz, C. C. (1992). Thought self-leadership: The influence of self-talk and mental imagery on performance. *Journal of organizational behavior*, 13(7), 681–699.

https://doi.org/10.1002/job.4030130705

www.ingramcontent.com/pod-product-compliance
Lightning Source LLC
Chambersburg PA
CBHW020859080526
44589CB00011B/363